Summer Countdown

Amy Puetz

Memory Making Stories & Activities for Five Summer Holidays

Golden Prairie Press
History at its Best!

Countdown Books by Amy Puetz

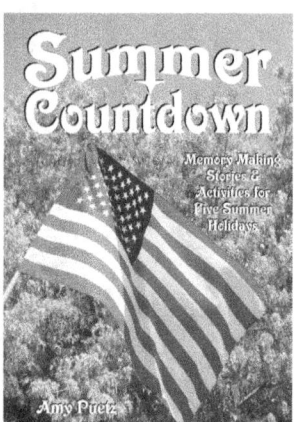

Available at www.AmyPuetz.com

Published by
Golden Prairie Press
P.O. Box 429
Wright, WY 82732
307-464-0266

www.AmyPuetz.com

Printed Book ISBN: 978-1-62492-022-6

Copyright 2015 by Amy Puetz
All Rights Reserved.

No part of this book may be reproduced in any form or by any electronic or mechanical means, including information storage and retrieval systems, without permission in writing from the author. The only exception is by a reviewer, who may quote short excerpts in a review.

Cover and Layout Design by Amy Puetz

Images from the Library of Congress, out of print books, www.army.mil, and Amy Puetz.

Contents

Introduction..1

Countdown to Mother's Day ~ Second Monday in May.........................2
Friday before Mother's Day..3
Borrowed Mothers by Carolyn Sherwin Bailey 3, Quotes by Abraham Lincoln and Martin Luther 6, Games for Mother's Day 7

Saturday before Mother's Day..8
The Only Son of His Mother by Florence Morse Kingsley 8, Quote by Richard Whately 10, Make a Mother's Day Card 13

Mother's Day..14
Cornelia's Jewels by James Baldwin 15, Quote by Jane Porter 15, The Two Windows by Carolyn Sherwin Bailey 16, Quotes by George Washington and Charles Dickens 16, Famous Mothers Quiz 17, Quote by Kate Douglas Wiggin 17

Countdown to Memorial Day ~ Last Monday in May..........................18
Saturday before Memorial Day...19
Two Heroes of the Civil War by Ben La Bree 19, Quote by General James Longstreet 20, Remembering 21

Sunday before Memorial Day...22
Three in a Gully by Arthur Willis Colton 22, Quote by James A. Garfield 25, "The Fallen" by John Vance Cheney 27, Heroes of the Civil War Quiz 28, "The Dead Volunteer" by J. W. Barker 28

Memorial Day...29
The Parshley Celebration by Sarah Orne Jewett 29, Memorial Day (decorate the grave of a soldier) 35, "Memorial Day" by Jane Campbell 35

Countdown to Flag Day ~ June 14...36
June 12...37
Our Flag's First Engagement by H. A. Ogden 37, Felt Flag Puzzle 40

June 13...42
The Little Victory by Dorothea Lay 42, "A Song for Our Flag" by Margaret E. Sangster 42, Flag of Betsy Ross by Harry Pringle Ford 43, Making a Five-Pointed Star 44

June 14 ~ Flag Day..45
Earning the Flag by Carolyn Sherwin Bailey 45, Song—"The Star Spangled Banner" 48

Countdown to Father's Day ~ Third Sunday in June..........................50
Friday before Father's Day...51
How the Home was Built by Maud Lindsay 51, "Daddies" by Edgar A. Guest 53, Make a Father's Day Card 54

Saturday before Father's Day...55
The Story of William Tell by James Hiram Fassett 56, "The Real Successes" by Edgar A. Guest 57, Letter to His Son by Theodore Roosevelt 58, Activities for Father's Day 59

Father's Day..60
The Prodigal Son retold by Jesse Lyman Hurlbut 61, Quote by Lydia Maria Francis Child 61, The Wise Father by Ernest Clark Hartwell 62, "The Man to Be" by Edgar A. Guest 62, Famous Fathers Quiz 63

Contents

Countdown to Independence Day ~ July 4..**64**

June 21..65
    A Famous Writing Desk by Albert Blaisdell 65, Signers—William Floyd 66, Francis Lewis 67, Philip Livingston 68, The Tricolor Game 69

June 22..70
    The Flag of Their Regiment by Carolyn Sherwin Bailey 70, Signers—Stephen Hopkins and John Penn 71, Samuel Adams 72, Samuel Huntington 73, Song—"Yankee Doodle" 75

June 23..76
    The General's Daughter by James Johonnot 77, Tempe Hides Her Horse by Mr. Blaisdell and Mr. Ball 78, Signers—Lewis Morris 78, William Ellery and Button Gwinnett 79, "Our Own Dear Land" by J. R. Thomas 80, Star Craft 80

June 24..82
    The Midnight Ride of Paul Revere by Henry Wadsworth Longfellow and Albert Blaisdell 82, Signers—Joseph Hewes and Caesar Rodney 83, Roger Sherman 84, Oliver Wolcott 85, William Williams 86, Motto of the American Revolution 86, Fruity Flag 87, Quotes by George Washington, Patrick Henry, and Benjamin Franklin 87

June 25..88
    The Quaker Patriot by Charles Morris 89, Burning Her House by Celina Eliza Means 92, Signers—George Read 89, Carter Braxton and John Hart 90, Robert Treat Paine 91, William Paca 92, Ladies Cap 93, Quote by Abigail Adams 93

June 26..94
    Putnam's Dashing Ride by James Baldwin 94, Signers—Thomas Stone 95, George Walton and John Morton 96, Quote by John Adams 96, Find the Cards 97

June 27..98
    Emily Geiger's Ride by Benson John Lossing 98, Signers—Thomas McKean 99, Richard Stockton 100, John Witherspoon 101, Charles Carroll and William Whipple 102, Quiz 102

June 28..103
    John Paul Jones by Albert Blaisdell 103, Signers—John Hancock 104, Abraham Clark and George Taylor 105, Cocked Hat 106

June 29..107
    Gold in the Bread by Albert Blaisdell 107, Signers—Elbridge Gerry 108, Lyman Hall and George Ross 109, Josiah Bartlett and George Clymer 110, Star Sandwiches 110, Quote by Josiah Bartlett 110

June 30..111
    On the Track of a Traitor by Charles Morris 111, Signers—Benjamin Harrison 112, Samuel Chase and Francis Hopkinson 113, Matthew Thornton 114, Thomas Nelson Jr. 116, Quotes by Hopkinson, Rush, and Wilson 117, Song —"America the Beautiful" 118

July 1..119
    The Rescue of a Redcoat by Grace E. Craig 119, Signers—Benjamin Franklin 121, William Hooper and James Smith 122, Benjamin Rush 123, Quotes by Benjamin Rush 124, Yankee Doodle Tunes Game 125

July 2..126
    An Escape from a Prison Ship by Everett Titsworth Tomlinson 126, Signers—Arthur Middleton and Francis Lightfoot Lee 128, James Wilson and Thomas Lynch Jr. 129, Robert Morris 130, Signers Quiz 131

July 3..132
    Tench Tilghman's Ride by Jams Baldwin 132, Signers—George Wythe 133, Richard Henry Lee 134, Edward Rutledge 135, Song—"My Country 'Tis of Thee" 137

July 4 ~ Independence Day..138
    The Rescue of Old Glory by Mrs. J. W. Wheeler 138, Signers—John Adams 139, Thomas Jefferson 140, Quote by Thomas Jefferson, Thomas Heyward Jr. 141, Racing for the Flag Game 142

Introduction

The summer months are usually busy with traveling, outdoor projects, and taking a break from school. There are many special holidays during the summer, and this book will help you celebrate those holidays through stories and activities. There are three days devoted to all the holidays except Independence Day. That one has a countdown of two weeks before July Fourth.

It is my sincere wish that this book will be used to create wonderful memories for you and your family. In our society, there are so many things that vie for our attention that we often don't spend time with those we love most. A hundred years ago things were very different. Families spent time in the evenings talking, reading, singing, and just fellowshipping. With the creation of the radio things changed and, when television became a staple in every home, the interaction between family members decreased even more. Now with computers, movies, and a myriad of other gadgets, families spend very little time building relationships. This book has a mission to help families grow closer together.

Before you jump into this book, I have a few things I'd like to say. The book is broken up into daily sections. Each day has a story and an activity that should take about 30 to 45 minutes. The story is first but feel free to change it around and start with the activity if it works best for you. Some of the activities (such as the cooking) may take more than the allotted time, so preview the activity before you get started. Also, if one of the activities doesn't sound like much fun, feel free to implement your own. If you have a special recipe you make every year, do this on one of the cooking days, or if you have a craft that you enjoy, do that on a craft day.

Nearly all the stories in this book were written in the 1800s and early 1900s, so some of the language may seem old fashioned. I have modernized some of the spelling, but I left most of the stories intact because the Victorian people had such a beautiful way of using words. It is always good to stretch our vocabulary. Many of these stories have not been reprinted since their first publication, and I'm so excited to share these with a whole new generation. Most of the stories can be used to help teach children important lessons. At the end of each story you could think of a few questions to ask your children, or maybe even have the children ask you questions!

Thank you for taking the time to read this introduction, and I pray that your family will grow closer to each other and to God during this summer.

Patriotic blessings,
Amy Puetz

Summer Countdown   **Amy Puetz**

Mother's Day
Second Sunday in May

A young girl of twelve bowed her head as her mother said a prayer at the end of their Sunday School class. They had been learning about the mothers of the Bible, and Mrs. Jarvis asked God to one day send someone to found a day to celebrate the influence of mothers. Anna Jarvis was young, but she remembered her mother's prayer and her mother's example. Anna was born during the War Between the States, but she loved to hear stories of how her mother had been a peacemaker between the people of Grafton, West Virginia. Their state had split away from Virginia in 1863 and joined the northern states during the Civil War. Discord ran high in West Virginia during and after the war, but Mrs. Jarvis planned a Mother's Friendship Day that would bring together people from both sides. Many people warned her that a riot may be the result, but Mrs. Jarvis went ahead. She gave a stirring speech that asked the veterans and families who lost loved ones to forgive and live together in peace. The meeting ended with all singing "Auld Lang Syne." Mrs. Jarvis had also started a Mother's Day Work Club before the war that taught people about sanitation and caring for the sick. When the war began, the clubs helped wounded soldiers. Mrs. Jarvis was a devoted Christian woman and taught Sunday School at the Andrews Methodist Episcopal Church for over twenty years.

The young girl who sat in the Sunday School class grew up and followed in the footsteps of her mother by helping to promote motherhood, even though she never married. Anna Jarvis wanted to bring her mother's dream of a national Mother's Day to life. Mrs. Jarvis died on May 9, 1905, and a few years later a celebration was held at the Andrews Methodist Episcopal Church in Grafton to commemorate her life. Anna wrote letters to national leaders promoting the idea of a national Mother's Day and eventually in 1914 President Woodrow Wilson signed a proclamation making it a national holiday.

The second Sunday in May was established as the official Mother's Day. During the early days, a white carnation would be given to people whose mothers were dead and a red one to those whose mothers were alive.

Friday before Mother's Day

Borrowed Mothers

By Carolyn Sherwin Bailey, 1918

"You'll surely come on Sunday, Mother, won't you?" Edith Wainwright bent over her mother's chair and put her arms around the slender figure in black. "There's going to be a special address and different music and, oh, everybody says our Greenlawn Mother's Day will be the best one we've ever had." Stopping for breath, Edith placed one hand on the pile of white linen that lay on Mrs. Wainwright's lap. "And there won't be anybody in the chorus with such a pretty dress as mine," she continued. "It was a good idea to have them all made in the same style, but mine is going to be handmade and hand embroidered. You'll finish it in time, won't you, Mother?"

Mrs. Wainwright looked up, a smile lighting her tired face. "Of course your dress will be ready, Dear. Haven't I over a week and every one of the evenings free for sewing? It has been a good deal of work, but I like to think that the dress you wear on Mother's Day will have so much of your own mother's handwork in it." She leaned back a second, pretending to look at the fine stitches she had just set, but in reality resting her eyes and flying fingers for a space.

The room looked like Edith. She had blown in like a wayward breeze, as happy and careless. A rug that she had tripped over lay in a heap, and dust from the street came in through the door that she had forgotten to close. Her books were scattered on the table, and she had tipped over a scrap basket in her haste to reach her mother. Edith was a loving, thoughtless girl. Her deep blue eyes were dark now with the affection she had for this mother of hers, but her mind was busy with other thoughts.

"I'm going to basketball practice now," she said. "I promised Frances I'd stop in to see her. I know I ought to do the lunch dishes, Mother. You haven't had time to finish them on account of the sewing, and I should get dinner, but I'm afraid I can't get home in time. You're coming on Mother's Day, aren't you, Dear? Frances wants us to find out how many mothers will be there so she can tell her father."

"I'll try," her mother looked down again at her work, the tired shadows in her face covering the smile. "But the house will need a thorough cleaning the last of the week, and Lonny's croup has kept me from sleeping very much lately, and—"

"Well, you'll try to come. I'll tell Frances that." Edith pulled her hat low over her curls and darted out through the door, looking like a bluebird in her dainty blue linen and crimson tie.

Her clear call at the big white gate of the parsonage had to be repeated. Edith waited quite a while before Frances, the minister's daughter, appeared, her white sweater over her arm and her brown eyes full of laughter.

"I thought I'd never get started," she said. "I promised Father that I'd dust the library for him one day this week, and he wants it done today. I just hate to do it—taking down all those musty old books and getting my nose full of dust. I got off, though, by coaxing, and then he is busy, and he hasn't any time to scold. He's beginning his sermon for Mother's Day. It's a nice short text, not a bit hard to remember. 'As one whom his mother comforteth, so will I comfort you.' Is your mother coming, Edith? I want to make out a list this afternoon if the girls can tell me."

"I don't know. She's been so busy since Father died; we haven't any maid now, you know. Lonny has been sick, and she is making me a dress, all by hand, to wear in the chorus. She said that she might be too tired to come," Edith answered. Both girls remained silent as they slowly made their way to the school gymnasium. At the door, Edith put her arm around Frances and whispered something in her ear.

Frances laughed. Then she hugged Edith and whispered something back to her. Both girls giggled.

"We always do think of the same things at just the same time, don't we, Frances?" Edith said.

"Yes, and always the nicest things!" Frances replied. "Now we'll have to see how the other girls feel about it."

The basketball practice for once lagged. Rumor flew about the gymnasium that Edith Wainwright and Frances Giddings had an idea, that it was a scheme with a plan attached, and they might share it when the game was over. So it was a few minutes before five when a merry, laughing throng of girls, led by Edith, put Frances on a kind of throne made of parallel bars and a mattress, and shouted, "Tell us about it, Frances! Please tell us!"

A flush of color rose to Frances' face, but she tossed her loosened hair back from her forehead and faced her mates with clear eyes.

"Maybe you'll laugh at us, girls," she began, "but Edith and I had the same idea come to us all at once, and we'd like to see if it will come to you too. I told Edith about the text father is going to preach on Mother's Day, 'As one whom his mother comforts, so will I comfort you.'"

Frances hesitated a moment, and her voice faltered. Then she bravely continued, "You see, I'd just run away from dusting Father's library—"

"And I'd left all the lunch dishes without washing them," Edith interrupted.

"So we decided to form a special club," Frances went on. "We plan to begin just as soon as we leave the gymnasium. We're going to have code names. They'll be very unusual code names, so it will make the society unusual and very nice we think. My codename is 'dust cloth.'"

"And mine is 'dishpan,'" Edith added with a decided nod of her curly head.

For a short space, there was silence in the gymnasium. A ripple of laughter at first was immediately hushed. Then the girls began to talk all at once.

"It's perfectly splendid, and we'll keep it up all the year."

"Nobody will ever find out about it and we can have hikes and sewing afternoons and picnics when we get through with the regular work of the club."

"My code name is going to be 'iron.'"

"Mine is 'broom.'"

"Mine is 'thimble.'"

The enthusiasm was contagious. Before ten minutes had passed, every girl in the basketball team had joined the club, and they scattered to begin making use of their new code names.

Frances and Edith went up the street arm in arm, in the glow of the yellow sunset.

"They wanted to do it, really; so did we, Edith," Frances said, "only they hadn't thought of it before. Neither had we thought of it." The sound of an automobile interrupted her, and the two girls saw a car coming down the tree-lined street toward them."

"There's Edward Judson," Edith said. "Doesn't he have just everything! His father lets him have his car and chauffeur almost every day after school. Hello, Edward!" She waved her hand to him.

The boy in the car motioned to the chauffeur to stop and took off his cap, a smile lighting his cheery, freckled face.

"I'm going over to the mill to get Dad and take him home," he said. "Jump in, girls, and we'll stop at the tea room and have a sundae."

"Goody. Maple walnut for me," Frances said.

"And chocolate peppermint for me!" Edith added as they drove off. It was at the little round table in the tea room, over the ice cream, that the girls told Edward about their new club, whispering it so that no one else could hear.

"It's fine!" Edward said as they went out. "I'd like to belong to it myself." He said goodbye to the girls and started off in the direction of the mill.

Frances turned to Edith when they were alone.

"I almost told Edward that he couldn't possibly belong," she said.

"I'm glad you stopped yourself in time," Edith said. "It would have made him feel bad. Being rich doesn't make up for not having any mother."

The week before Mother's Day went by on wings. The newly formed club astonished its mothers by doing things at home cheerfully that they had grumbled about before or neglected altogether. Edith decided to wear her last year's white dress in the chorus so that her mother might have some evenings of rest, and she amused fretting little Lonny and made good use of her code name. Dr. Giddings found his library neatly dusted. The other girls got up early without being called and played seamstress and waitress and kitchen maid and gardener, with the result that the mothers of Greenlawn could hardly understand the change in their daughters. But it was a comfort to be able to rest weary feet and hands and get ready for Mother's Day.

The day was a most lovely one. The girls were bubbling over with happiness, for their work had been made merry by its secrecy. It had been such fun to give the code names in school and mystify the boys, who could not seem to understand their significance. The boys and girls in Greenlawn Grammar School were particularly good friends. The girls were apt to attend the baseball matches in a body and bring sandwiches and ice-cold lemonade of their own making. The boys, in return, were always ready to put up swings for a picnic or shift scenes for a school play.

"I believe the boys are a little bit hurt because we haven't let them in our club," Frances said to her father as they walked beneath the leafy bower of the trees toward the little gray stone church on Mother's Day. "But what could they have done in it? We've never done anything before without Edward, but he hasn't any mother."

The minister put his hand on his beloved daughter's shoulder.

"So many in the world have no mothers," he said, "but that is one reason we have this day. We want to share our mother love, and mother care, and mother spirit." Then he suddenly stopped, putting on his eyeglasses as he looked up the street.

"What is that?" he asked. "Look, Frances, it seems to be a kind of procession."

It was a procession of boys, but they were not alone. Heading it was an automobile full of old ladies. They had each a bright corsage pinned to their shabby black frocks, and they were rivaling the day in the sunshine of their smiles. Following were more old ladies carefully escorted by boys. All had bouquets, and the boys wore their best suits and their very best manners.

"It's our boys!" Frances exclaimed. "They're stopping at the church."

The two hastened and reached the churchyard just as Edward got out of the car and opened the door to let out his party of delighted guests. The other boys ushered their charges in the gate, pretending not to notice the girls, but addressing strange words to each other.

"Wood basket!"

"Grocery list!"

"Clothes line!"

Edward was the most mystifying of all. He said "Green tea" in an undertone to Edith as he helped a particularly old lady of his automobile party up the church steps. Moreover, the mothers of the boys, who had come earlier, seemed to be in the secret too, for they could be seen nodding and laughing to one another. Each one wore a beautiful bouquet of flowers and a particularly happy expression.

Frances looked up laughingly into her father's face.

"Code names!" she said. "The boys got even with us. You see, our club is to have a Mother's Day at home every day, but we didn't tell the boys about it, except for Edward.

> All that I am or ever hope to be, I owe to my angel mother.
> ~Abraham Lincoln
>
> Earth has nothing more tender than a woman's heart, when it is the abode of piety.
> ~Martin Luther

They always say they can do things just as well as we can. Edward must have told them, and they've not only done all that we have done, but they've brought all the old ladies from the Poor Farm."

The minister stood beside the gate, his hat off as the last of the boys' borrowed mothers went inside. Their eyes were dim from a great many years of watching, their fingers were twisted and bent from the toil that had gone without its reward, leaving only the scars. But they had shining faces, and not one was without a corsage or a boy to escort her to church.

The music of the prelude poured out of the door, and in a tree in the churchyard a mother bird sang above her nest.

"Wasn't it nice of the boys?" Frances said as she joined Edith.

"As one whom his mother comforts!" Her father said, going inside. "Every one of them comforted!"

Games for Mother's Day
By Mary Dawson, 1916

1 Find photographs, either as children or young girls, of all the mothers to be entertained. Display them on cards that you have numbered. Distribute pencils and papers and let the company guess "who's who?" writing down the answers as they suppose them to be identified with the numbers. If you do not have a large group, you might pick some historically important mothers and have everyone guess who they are, such as the ones pictured at right. They are: (1) Philippa of Hainault, mother of the Black Prince; (2) Mary Ball, mother of George Washington; (3) Anne Boleyn, mother of Queen Elizabeth I.

2 Write out a list of the maiden names of mothers present and see who can guess which is which.

3 Write out twelve quotations concerning motherhood selected from any good book of quotations. See who can guess the authors' names, or omit the last word of each quotation and have the guests add these to the best of their ability. Visit www.AmyPuetz.com/mothers.html for a list of quotes.

Saturday before Mother's Day

The Only Son of His Mother

By Florence Morse Kingsley, 1903
Author of Titus, a Comrade of the Cross

Perched halfway up the hillside, and overhung with green branches like a bird's nest, was the house—little and low and old, its moss-grown, earthen roof, pretty in springtime with a myriad of blossoms, which flaunted their bright silken heads in the soft air. Later, the great plain beneath would send up parching heat, and the steady, unwinking stare of the sun would parch the clay roof until it was bare and brown as the active hands of Anna, who toiled from dawn until evening in house and garden.

Far below lay the vast level stretches of the Jezreel Valley, studded with blossoming groves and orchards, and flecked with wandering droves of cloud-shadows. Above straggled the steep, irregular streets of the village, half-hidden among luxuriant gardens and vineyards, and guarded by an ancient wall, ruinous and decayed, but still boasting the dignity of a gate on the east and one on the west. These gates were duly opened at sunrise and closed at sunset, to the satisfaction of the inhabitants, who had thus maintained the name and state of a city through uncounted generations.

To Anna, cheerful and busy in her own little nest of a house, with its well-ordered garden, its triple rows of grapevines, and its half score of olives and pomegranate trees, it mattered little that a daily miracle of beauty was performed before her eyes. The wide meadows of the Jezreel Valley, green as lucent emerald in the warm springtime, gold in summer, and purple with brooding mists in the bleak winter days, held for her but one interest. Her child was there. Joshua, the son of Anna, had done man's work for the rich wine merchant, Resen, for the space of six and thirty moons.

"He is a well-grown lad—is my son," Anna would boast to the women who gathered at the fountain with their pitchers, "a well-grown lad and industrious beyond belief. Find for me a thistle in my bit of a vineyard or a weed in my bed of herbs! Come, I will pay any one of you a silver penny for a single leaf! And never a coin of his wage that does not find its way to my hand!" Then she would nod her head and show her white teeth with a smile of pride and joy.

As for the neighbors, they did not grudge a word of praise for the lad. Was he not the only son of his mother—and she a widow? He was a handsome boy, moreover, with a ready laugh like his mother's and was well liked on his own account. Already there was talk of a marriage between the widow's son and Tirzah, the prettiest maid in the village. It was reported that the matter of dowry was as good as settled, and that Tirzah would be sewing the wedding tallith (prayer shawl) before winter.

"It is true that I have been sorely afflicted," Anna often added at such times, "more, I may say, than any one of you." This last with a mournful pride as of one who has been distinguished and set apart in a notable manner. "Who of you all, I ask, has lost a husband, and after him—one—two—three sons and a daughter? Rachel, yonder, can tell you that my eyes were all but blind with weeping, and my voice gone from me with shrilling for the departed. For all left me in a twelvemonth, treading, as it were, upon one another's heels in their haste to be gone. Then there was but the one, Joshua, and he a wailing babe. I had scarce spirit to hold him in these arms."

"But he was always a fine child!" put in old Rachel, wagging her withered forefinger. "Did I not tell you even in those days that all was not over for you?"

"You have spoken!" cried the widow exultantly, her quick-glancing dark eyes filling with tears of joy. "There was never a finer child from the first day of his breath until now. I have said a thousand times—and I say it once more in the presence of you all—that Jehovah has repaid me. Now what, may I ask, can many children advantage one if they are lean and sickly, or if they are forward and disobedient, idle, and given to drinking wine, and gluttony? Is not one like to my son better than a score of such?"

In the fields of Resen, the rich wine merchant, the widow's son toiled from dawn until evening every day, except the Sabbath day, and he pleased his master right well. If any lingered in the pleasant shade of the tamarisk trees in the hot noontides beyond the appointed time, Resen might be sure that the son of Anna was not among them. Yet it was true that it was sometimes difficult for one to fall diligently to work at the exact moment when the black shadow of the noon-stone fell crossways the green line set up by Resen to mark the limit of the rest hour. And this more especially when the mighty Ben Hazar was relating marvelous stories out of the Talmud and the Mishnah, for Ben Hazar was of near kin to a rabbi and therefore had learning.

Many of these strange stories had to do with the long-expected Messiah of Israel, and young Joshua's heart beat loud in his bosom when on one such occasion Ben Hazar assured them that the great rabbi, Ben Jothan, his kinsman, had declared in his hearing, not three moons since, that there were rumors abroad, in the regions of Galilee of a strange new prophet, one Jesus of Nazareth, who had performed wonders beyond the power of mortal man. Water had been turned into wine at a wedding feast in Cana; lepers and paralytic folk had been healed; devils—both mute and speaking, had been cast out, with other marvels past the telling.

"It is still a question," Ben Hazar had added, pursing up his mouth judicially and frowning—as was the manner of the rabbi, his kinsman—"as to whether this man Jesus is not himself devil-possessed, assuredly, and therefore able to dominate the lesser forces of evil at work among men. I have myself known a sorcerer—one Simon Bar Jesus—who was able to cure the evil eye."

"Did this man, Simon Bar Jesus, heal lepers also?" demanded Joshua, his brown cheeks flushed crimson with excitement.

Ben Hazar drew his grizzled brows together. "I never heard that he did. For myself, I must needs look into this matter of the Nazarene with my own eyes. Tomorrow, I shall not come to the vineyard; I shall go instead to Capernaum. The man is there today, tomorrow, and it may be longer. Assuredly I shall have the worth of my wage if I but behold a miracle!"

"And you will see him?" whispered the lad, half under his breath. A sudden desire had sprung up in his heart, potent, irresistible. If only he might see this wonderful man—this Jesus of Nazareth! He resolved to lay the matter before his mother.

In the garden that evening when the sun had sunk behind the violet range of mountains, Joshua told his mother of the man, Jesus of Nazareth. "I wish to see him, Mother," he said when he had repeated all that Ben Hazar had related under the tamarisk trees. "Let me go tomorrow to find him. He is in Capernaum."

Anna threw up her hands with an exclamation of displeasure. "Capernaum!" she cried. "Surely you are losing your wits, Son. Capernaum is more than a day's journey from here—more than a score of miles!"

"But I could go and return, Mother, between dawn and evening," pleaded the lad. "If only I might see him!"

"Think no more of the matter," interposed the woman, raising her voice. "Have I not boasted myself openly that my son is no idler; and shall I see you waste a whole day—nay, more likely two—and lose your wage, that you may run after a prophet? Not so."

Then observing the boy's downcast face, and thinking to herself that he was no longer a child, she went on in a tone of beseeching, "Listen to me now, my son—for

> A mother once asked a clergyman when she should begin the education of her child, which she told him was then four years old. "Madam," was the reply, "you have lost three years already. From the very first smile that gleams over an infant's cheek, your opportunity begins."
> ~Richard Whately

although I am but your mother I have yet a little wisdom, together with much love. I also have heard of this Nazarene; at the fountain he has been spoken of, and in the marketplace. He is not Messiah, but only a carpenter, the son of a carpenter, who has worked with his hands for many years.

"Nay, he is no more and no better than you are, lord of my house! These are but idle tales. Ben Hazar is a spreader of great, swollen fables, as all the world knows.

"Hear also what I shall tell you, Son. I have in the strong box within—how much, do you think? A hundred pence—lacking but seven pieces! When the seven shall be added, I go straightway to the mother of Tirzah and demand her for you. And now will you idle away two or three days to run after the son of a carpenter, eh? Bring me the seven pence, Lad, and you shall have a holiday indeed!"

Joshua looked down at his strong brown hands in silence. He loved his mother; also he had a great, though secret, tenderness for the beautiful young maid of whom his mother had spoken. Yet stronger than either—though why he knew not—was this newborn desire to see the wonderful stranger. Seven pence—and they stood between him and a sight of Jesus of Nazareth!

On the following morning, he found Resen, the master of the vineyard, in an angry humor. "That lazy fool, Ben Hazar, is again absent!" he cried. "Sacred blood, but I could beat him with this staff until my arm dropped at my side! And who now will haul up the buckets from the river today—and the vines parching with drought?"

The labor of hauling up the heavy buckets with the slow-turning windlass was terrible; the absent Ben Hazar was a giant in strength and performed it easily. The other laborers eyed the motionless wheel solemnly. No one offered himself for the task.

Resen frowned more angrily than ever. "Lazy hands, all!" he cried loudly, turning his back upon them. "And you know right well that the wage is double what you can earn amongst the vines."

Joshua started forward. "Two pence?" he asked timidly. "Is it two pence that you will pay?"

Resen regarded him sourly. "Two pence—yes; I have said it. Can you do it?"

"Yes," said Joshua firmly, "I will do it."

Some of the others shrugged their shoulders as they turned away. They knew that Ben Hazar received four pence for every day that he worked from dawn until sunset. But this, in truth, concerned none of them.

The work was hard, terribly hard. Before noon the boy's hands were blistered, and every fiber of his young body ached with fatigue; but the thought that in four days he should be the possessor of eight pence nerved him to the task.

"I will have a holiday," he said to himself, "I will find Jesus of Nazareth." Also he thought shyly of Tirzah, with her soft black eyes, and her cheeks, brown and softly dimpled like the shifting surface of the fountain. Only seven pence between him and all this happiness!

That night he was too weary to eat his supper, and afterward tossed and moaned loudly in his sleep, so that Anna crept to his side three times to lay her cool fingers on his forehead.

"It is the heat of the sun," she murmured anxiously. "He ought, perhaps, to rest a day in the shade."

But the next morning found the lad eager for his task. "I must make haste, my mother," he said, smiling into her troubled face, "to fetch the seven pence. Afterward, remember, I am to have a holiday."

"A holiday!" cried Anna. "Ah, so sets the wind! Aye, a holiday and a bride for you, my son. Garlands also and feasting—even the feast of betrothal!"

It was this, she thought, which ailed the lad and kept him from sleeping quietly, and her glad fancy ran nimbly forward into the years which lay before. A betrothal; a wedding—ah, such a wedding, with dancing and music and feasting! And the whole village at the doors to praise and bless the bride and throw handfuls of flowers and parched grain at the feet of the handsome bridegroom. Later there would be the sound of children's voices in the little house, sons and daughters once more under the old roof. "Truly Jehovah has been good to me," she sang. "I will praise Him with my whole heart!"

Meanwhile, Joshua, in the damp, exhausting heat of the plain below, toiled ceaselessly at the windlass. As the slow hours passed, the creaking chain sang in his ears a strange song, and the figures of the laborers, passing and repassing among the crowded ranks of vines, loomed up vast and unsubstantial as the figures in a dream.

"Fool, you are no longer filling the buckets!" shouted Resen, angrily raising his staff. Then he swore a great oath and stood stock still, staring with bulging eyes. The straining figure at the wheel wavered and sank sideways to the ground, the creaking chain rasped and spluttered harshly in its rapid descent to the river while the clumsy wooden handle of the windlass, thicker than a man's arm, smote the prostrate figure twice—three—four times with a dull crash.

They stared at him stupidly as he lay motionless in the hot sunshine, a thin stream of blood making its slow way amongst the parched and dusty weeds at their feet.

"Why do you stand there like speechless cattle?" cried Resen, recovering himself suddenly. "You are my witnesses that this day's work is none of my doing! Pick him up, you, Dan and Abel! Take him away to his house."

And so they brought him to his mother. He breathed through that day and night, slowly, painfully. At dawn he opened his eyes. They were misty with swift-approaching death. "I shall see him!" he cried faintly, and with the cry his soul passed.

Anna had sat at his side through the long hours like a statue—soundless, motionless. But at the voice of that cry she fell forward on her face.

At the hour between high noon and the setting of the sun on that same day, as was the custom, they carried him forth to his burial. His young face, upturned to the blue sky, was both sweet and smiling; on his heart lay three lilies, dropped there by the fairest maid in all the village, Tirzah, her dark eyes swollen with weeping, and all the dimpling laughter fled from her brown cheeks. Beside the green-garlanded bier tottered Anna, blind with grief, crazed with anguish. "My son, my son!" she moaned feebly, the strident shrilling of the flutes and the mournful wailing of the women falling unheeded on her dull ears.

Down the long, straggling street of the village passed the little procession, and all the people, both young and old, seeing it, burst into loud cries of grief, and, dropping their various vocations, followed the corpse.

"Alas! Alas!" they cried. "Alas! For the young man in his strength! Alas! For the tree cut down before the day of his fruitage! Alas! For the desolate woman! Surely Jehovah has smitten—has stricken her. With sore affliction has he bowed her to the ground, like a vine that is withered!"

And now befell a strange thing—assuredly the strangest thing in all the weary tale of earth's sorrows. Uncounted mothers have wept despairingly over their dead. During unnumbered centuries have blue summer skies looked down upon the living as they fold their dead away in darkness. Yet on this one day, as the mourning villagers passed from out their eastern gate along the dusty highway which led to Capernaum, another procession met them. Life eternal and death confronted each other there.

As to what followed, was it not written long ago in the annals of an ancient Book? These are all the words of it, "And it came to pass that he went into a city called Nain, and many of his disciples went with him, and many people. Now when he came nigh to the gate of the city, behold, there was a dead man carried out, the only son of his mother, and she was a widow, and many people of the city were with her. And when the Lord saw her, he had compassion on her and said unto her, 'Weep not.' And he came and touched the bier, and they that bare him stood still. And he said, 'Young man, I say unto you, Arise.' And he that was dead sat up, and began to speak. And he delivered him to his mother." (Luke 7:11-17).

Make a Mother's Day Card

Copy this page and color it. Fold an 8½ by 11 sheet of colored card stock in half and glue the colored picture to it. Write a nice note inside the card and sign it. Give it to your mother on Sunday.

Happy Mother's Day

Summer Countdown — Amy Puetz

Mother's Day

Cornelia's Jewels
By James Baldwin, 1896

The Two Windows
By Carolyn Sherwin Bailey, 1918

Cornelia's Jewels
By James Baldwin, 1896

It was a bright morning in the old city of Rome many hundred years ago. In a vine-covered summerhouse in a beautiful garden, two boys were standing. They were looking at their mother and her friend who were walking among the flowers and trees.

"Did you ever see so handsome a lady as our mother's friend?" asked the younger boy, tugging at his tall brother's hand. "She looks like a queen."

"Yet she is not so beautiful as our mother," said the elder boy. "She has a fine dress, it is true, but her face is not noble and kind. It is our mother who is like a queen."

"That is true," said the other. "There is no woman in Rome so much like a queen as our dear mother."

Soon Cornelia, their mother, came down the walk to speak with them. She was simply dressed in a plain white robe. Her arms and feet were bare, as was the custom in those days, and no rings nor chains glittered about her hands and neck. For her only crown, long braids of soft brown hair were coiled about her head, and a tender smile lit up her noble face as she looked into her sons' proud eyes.

"Boys," she said, "I have something to tell you."

They bowed before her, as Roman lads were taught to do, and said, "What is it, Mother?"

"You are to dine with us today, here in the garden, and then our friend is going to show us that wonderful casket of jewels of which you have heard so much."

The brothers looked shyly at their mother's friend. Was it possible that she had still other rings besides those on her fingers? Could she have other gems besides those which sparkled in the chains about her neck?

When the simple outdoor meal was over, a servant brought the casket from the house. The lady opened it. Ah, how those jewels dazzled the eyes of the wondering boys! There were ropes of pearls, white as milk and smooth as satin; heaps of shining rubies, red as the glowing coals; sapphires as blue as the sky that summer day; and diamonds that flashed and sparkled like the sunlight. The brothers looked long at the gems.

"Ah!" whispered the younger, "if our mother could only have such beautiful things!"

At last, however, the casket was closed and carried carefully away.

"Is it true, Cornelia, that you have no jewels?" asked her friend. "Is it true, as I have heard it whispered, that you are poor?"

"No, I am not poor," answered Cornelia, and as she spoke, she drew her two boys to her side, "for here are my jewels. They are worth more than all your gems."

I am sure that the boys never forgot their mother's pride and love and care, and in after years, when they had become great men in Rome, they often thought of this scene in the garden. And the world still likes to hear the story of Cornelia's jewels.

> In the career of female fame, there are few prizes to be obtained which can vie with the obscure state of a beloved wife or a happy mother.
> ~Jane Porter

The Two Windows
By Carolyn Sherwin Bailey, 1918

Once upon a time, in a country far away from here, there were two windows. One looked out on the village street, for it was a cottage window, and one looked over the sea and the plains, for it was a tower window.

One day a painter came to that country, and he walked through the village street and up, up the hill until he came to the tower. He wanted to find a high place where he could set his easel and see the plains and the sea and the sunrise and the sunset, and paint a more beautiful picture than any that he had ever painted before. So he climbed the tower stairs, and he looked out from the tower window.

Yes, it was a very wonderful picture that he saw. The other hills lay all green and gold before his eyes, and the sea sparkled blue as a turquoise. But what was that? Way, way off in the valley, so far away that he could not paint it, was a spot of bright gold color. Then it changed to rose and then to amethyst. Never in all his life had the painter seen such a pretty bit of color. He must go nearer to it. He must see what lay all about it.

He strapped his easel to his back and started down toward the valley and the wonderful bit of color. It was a long, long way, but he kept on, never tiring, and always with the patch of color in front of him.

Presently it led him into the village and then down the village street. Then he found it. It was the little cottage window with the sunset reflected in its polished panes.

As the painter stopped before the little window that shone so bright and prettily, he peered inside. It was all quite poor, but so neat and tidy! In a corner of the cottage room, a mother was rocking a baby to sleep and singing softly as she swayed to and fro in a little, old red chair.

"I have found the prettiest picture in the world," said the painter, and he took out his brushes and his colors and began to paint.

My mother was the most beautiful woman I ever saw. All I am I owe to my mother. I attribute all my success in life to the oral, intellectual, and physical education I received from her. ~George Washington

**I think it must somewhere be written that the virtues of mothers shall, occasionally, be visited on their children, as well as the sins of the fathers.
~Charles Dickens**

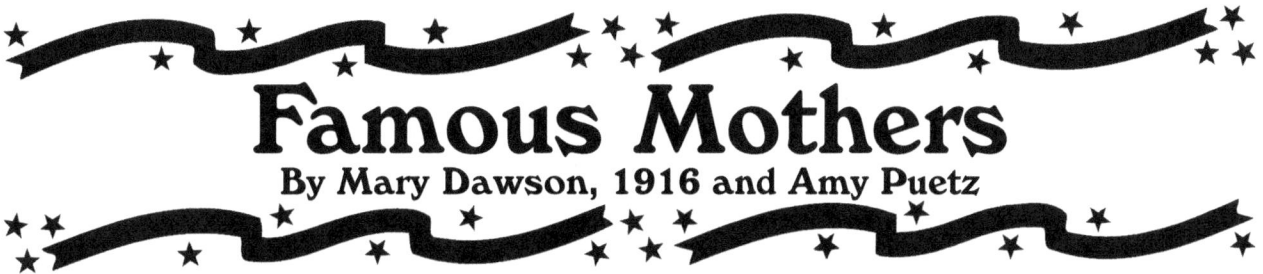

Famous Mothers
By Mary Dawson, 1916 and Amy Puetz

Test your knowledge of the mothers behind famous men. Match the question on the left with the correct woman on the right. Answers are below.

1. What was George Washington's mother's maiden name?
2. What Roman mother called her children her jewels?
3. What mother disciplined her infant a few months old and taught him "to cry softly"?
4. What celebrated mother of a great emperor made a renowned journey to the Holy Land at seventy-five years of age?
5. What great queen was the mother of another queen who was killed during the French Revolution?
6. This mother who lived in Egypt saved her baby by putting him in a basket in the Nile River.
7. What great doctor of the Church was reclaimed from sin largely through the efforts and prayers of his saintly mother?
8. What was Abraham Lincoln's mother's maiden name?

A. Jochebed
B. Mary Ball
C. St. Helena, mother of Constantine the Great
D. Maria Theresa of Austria, mother of Marie Antoinette
E. Cornelia
F. Nancy Hanks
G. St. Augustine, whose mother was St. Monica
H. Susanna Wesley, mother of John

Answers 1-B, 2-E, 3-H, 4-C, 5-D, 6-A, 7-G, 8-F

Only One Mother

Most of all the other beautiful things in life come by twos and threes, by dozens and hundreds. Plenty of roses, stars, sunsets, rainbows, brothers, and sisters, aunts and cousins, but only one mother in the whole world.
~Kate Douglas Wiggin

Memorial Day
Last Monday in May

After the dark days of the American Civil War women began decorating the graves of their lost loved ones. On May 5, 1868, Major General John A. Logan, who was the head of the Union veterans, said that graves should be decorated on May 30. The holiday became known as Decoration Day. The first large event was held at Arlington National Cemetery. General Grant presided over the ceremony, and people went through the cemetery singing hymns, saying prayers, and putting flowers on the graves of Confederate and Union soldiers.

Although the very first observance of Decoration Day is not known, local tradition says that, in April of 1866 southern women in Columbus, Mississippi placed flowers on the graves of those who died at Shiloh. The idea spread and by the late 1860s many cities celebrated Decoration Day. After World War I, Decoration Day was set aside to honor all those who had died fighting for their country.

The holiday became known as Memorial Day over the years and was meant to be a time to remember those who gave "the last full measure of their devotion." In 1971, the last Monday in May was set aside as Memorial Day and declared a national holiday by an act of Congress.

Many southern states also have their own days for honoring the Confederate dead. Mississippi celebrates Confederate Memorial Day on the last Monday of April, Alabama on the fourth Monday of April, and Georgia on April 26. North and South Carolina observe it on May 10, Louisiana on June 3, and Tennessee calls that date Confederate Decoration Day. Texas celebrates Confederate Heroes Day January 19 and Virginia calls the last Monday in May Confederate Memorial Day.

Saturday before Memorial Day

Two Heroes of the Civil War

By Ben La Bree, 1914

Bravery Honored by a Foe
By Ben La Bree, 1914

In a rifle pit, on the brow of a hill near Fredericksburg, were a number of Confederate soldiers who had exhausted their ammunition in the vain attempt to check the advancing column of Hooker's finely equipped and disciplined army which was crossing the river. To the relief of these few came the brigade in double-quick time. But no sooner were the soldiers entrenched than the firing on the opposite side of the river became terrific.

A heavy mist obscured the scene. The Federal soldiers poured a merciless fire into the trenches. Soon many Confederates fell, and the agonized cries of the wounded who lay there calling for water smote the hearts of their helpless comrades.

"Water! Water!" But there was none to give; the canteens were empty.

"Boys," exclaimed Nathan Cunningham, a lad of eighteen, the color bearer for his regiment, "I can't stand this any more. They want water, and water they must have. So let me have a few canteens, and I'll go for some."

Carefully laying the colors, which he had borne on many a field, in a trench, he seized some canteens, and, leaping into the mist, was soon out of sight.

Shortly after this the firing ceased for a while, and an order came for the men to fall back to the main line.

As the Confederates were retreating, they met Nathan Cunningham, his canteens full of water, hurrying to relieve the thirst of the wounded men in the trenches. He glanced over the passing column and saw that the faded flag, which he had carried so long, was not there. The men, in their haste to obey orders, had forgotten or overlooked the colors.

Quickly, the lad sped to the trenches, intent now not only on giving water to his comrades, but on rescuing the flag and in order to save the honor of his regiment.

His mission of mercy was soon accomplished. The wounded men drank freely. The lad then found and seized his colors and turned to rejoin his regiment. Scarcely had he gone three paces when a company of Federal soldiers appeared ascending the hill.

"Halt and surrender," came the stern command, and a hundred rifles were leveled at the boy's breast.

"Never while I hold the colors," was his firm reply.

The morning sun, piercing with a lurid glare the dense mist, showed the lad proudly standing with his head thrown back and his flag grasped in his hand, while his unprotected breast was exposed to the fire of his foe.

A moment's pause. Then the Federal officer gave his command, "Back with your pieces, men, don't shoot that brave boy."

And Nathan Cunningham, with colors flying over his head, passed on and joined his regiment. His comrades in arms told with pride of his brave deed and the generous act of a foe.

The broad, deep Americanism which pulses through the great heart of the Republic today will grow broader and deeper with the passing years. I am thankful that I have lived to see this noble result of the war springing into vast and virile life. The passions of the titanic struggle will finally enter upon the sleep of oblivion, and only its splendid accomplishments for the cause of human freedom and a united nation, stronger and richer in patriotism because of the great strife, will be remembered.
~ General James Longstreet, Confederate Officer

Bravery of Richard Kirtland
By Ben La Bree, 1914

Richard Kirtland was a sergeant in the Second Regiment of South Carolina Volunteers. The day after the great battle of Fredericksburg, Kershaw's brigade occupied the road at the foot of Marye's Hill.

One hundred and fifty yards in front of the road, on the other side of a stone wall, lay Sykes' division of the United States Army. Between these troops and Kershaw's command, a skirmish continued through the entire day. The ground between the lines was literally covered with dead and dying Federal soldiers.

All day long the wounded were calling, "Water! Water! Water!"

In the afternoon, Sergeant Kirtland, a Confederate soldier, went to the headquarters of General Kershaw, and said with deep emotion, "General, all through last night and today I have been hearing those poor wounded Federal soldiers out there crying for water. Let me go and give them some."

"Don't you know," replied the general, "that you would get a bullet through you the moment you stepped over the wall?"

"Yes, sir," said the sergeant, "but if you will let me go I am willing to try it."

The general reflected a minute, then answered, "Kirtland, I ought not to allow you to take this risk, but the spirit that moves you is so noble I cannot refuse. Go, and may God protect you!"

In the face of almost certain death, the sergeant climbed the wall, watched with anxiety by the soldiers of his army. Under the curious gaze of his foes, and exposed to their fire, he dropped to the ground and hastened on his errand of mercy. Unharmed, untouched, he reached the nearest sufferer. He knelt beside him, tenderly raised his drooping head, rested it gently on his chest, and poured the cooling life-giving water down the parched throat. This done he laid him carefully down, placed the soldier's knapsack under his head, straightened his broken limbs, spread his coat over him, replaced the empty canteen with a full one, then turned to another sufferer.

By this time, his conduct was understood by friend and foe alike and the firing ceased on both sides.

For an hour and a half, he pursued his noble mission until he had relieved the wounded in all parts of the battlefield. Then he returned to his post uninjured. Surely such a noble deed is worthy of the admiration of men and angels.

Remembering
By Amy Puetz

Ask your parents and grandparents about veterans in your family who served in past wars. Here are some questions you could ask. What was their rank? Where did they serve? Did they serve during peacetime or in a war? What was it like being a soldier?

As you listen to their stories, remember the sacrifice that our military makes so that we can stay free. Are any of them still alive? Is there something you could do to thank them for their service?

Sunday before Memorial Day

Three in a Gully
By Arthur Willis Colton, 1921

There was a long row of cottages above the beach, and beyond the beach was the sea, and then the sea forever, except for Lackland Island, floating a mile offshore like a water lily. At evening, we came to the colonel's porch to see the scenery. Little Peggy McLean sighed with satisfaction and said, "Now tell us about heroes."

"Ah, the heroes!" said the colonel, a gentlemen through and through and, therefore, not afraid to reveal his sentiments. "There were enough of them, but not all were heroes. Some died because they were afraid."

Old Judge Dudley, all huddled up with rheumatism, although his eyes were yet clear and keen, crept tremulously across to the colonel's cottage when he saw the gathering, because he liked to see what was going on and hear the talk.

"I believe you, colonel," said the judge then. "That's a historic country—the Tennessee Valley and northward. I'm Connecticut-born. I like to see any man smack of his soil and believe it's the best place on God's earth. Yes, Sir, I like that."

Peggy McLean, who was chewing taffy, opened her sticky mouth and again demanded heroes. And the colonel told his tale, pulling his gray mustache whenever the story moved him, and looking down on the shiny sea where the surf murmured.

"Now, Peggy, you can't have all heroes, just some common folk among them. Same as if you have taffy all the time, you would despise it. But taffy is good, and heroes are good, but not all the time."

He whistled reflectively, and Peggy looked at the taffy, feeling herself to be a sinner. The colonel went on gently:

"I'm not saying anything of heroes today, only a couple of common men and a dog, I being one. I was one of the men, Peggy, not the dog. He was just a pup, but he was clever. And I'm not to tell you about battles and campaigns, though there is one thing about campaigns that only the poor soldier understands. It is this: that his legs are so tired it makes the heart sick to think of them. I am to tell of something nearby and after a battle, namely of Lookout Mountain to the south in Tennessee, which you've all been badgered into learning at school, I reckon, and have your own ideas about.

"I'd like you to notice that it's a powerful steep mountain to climb, and it's risky getting down in a hurry. And maybe you remember that we Confederates had to get off the top on account of the Federals coming up the other side and acting like hornets. That was surely a fact.

"They say the retreat was orderly as could be, considering the ground; but in some places it was scattery, and besides, when the top was lost it was no good waiting, and one might as well be at the bottom in a hurry. Just how it happened, and so unnoticed, I don't know, but the roar of the musketry and the trampling and the high wind were great; and going somewhat to the southward, though not thinking to be far apart, I fell over a log and into a little thicket of brambles on a slope that dropped off at the end with a plunge.

"It was all done quickly and too quietly in the uproar; and after that I had nothing more to do with the battle of Lookout Mountain, or of Missionary Ridge, either, though I remember the low moan of the cannonading throughout the next two days somewhere off to the east. There was a little brook going somewhere near us in the gully, and that and the cannonading were both sleepy sounds. I can shut my eyes and hear them now. The cannons say, 'Oh, oh, oh,' and the brook says, 'Oo, oo, oo!'

"So I was not wounded at the battle of Lookout Mountain like a soldier and a gentleman, but fell into a gully out of foolishness and broke my leg.

"The gully was a slit cut in the face of the mountain, the sides of it steep and stony, and perhaps forty feet high; and it was a twisted gully, so that I could not see far above or below, and I lay as if in a hole in the ground.

"I don't know what happened first after the plunge, only I reckon to have hit my head somewhere and fallen in a heap at the bottom, and there I found myself after a time, crumpled up and bumped all over, and my leg one big pain.

"I didn't care for anything else just then, for in the first place it is not interesting when your men are going the wrong way. If they had been going up instead of down, I should have been hot to be with them, but as it was I only wanted someone else to fall into the gully and set my leg. I thought maybe someone else would, and I shouldn't have minded advising him to fall some other way from the way I fell. I was all ready to own up it was a poor way.

"The cracking of the rifles went on irregularly—sometimes a roar, and then only here and there. But the trampling and shouting were dying away down the mountain, so I knew that no friends of mine were any longer near. Next I heard an odd sound for that place—the barking of a dog—and then a sound that was in that place a common one and much to be expected, the sharp cry of a wounded man on the rocks above.

"He came straight down with a thud and a roll, but he was in no shape to set my leg, though he fell right near. He was hurt in the shoulder or chest, but I could not tell how badly. He lay white and still, the blood running across his hand, and I knew it was my job to do for him, Federal or not. Federal he was, and a small man and young, in a blue coat.

"That common little pup kept yelping on the rocks overhead to show he was interested, and presently, he tried to pick his way down, and slipped and slid and yelped louder on account of losing skin. Then he came along the bottom, sniffing at the little Federal and looking kind of put out when he saw what shape he was in. But he seemed kind of glad to find I was tolerably alive and snuggled up to me. He, sniffing and moaning all the time, looked at the little Federal, seeming to say, 'My, ain't that too bad!'

"So there we were, we three ordinary folks whom the great war had thrown aside and left in a kind of wrinkle of an old mountain—just as when a sea more than commonly high throws some bits of weed up the beach there and goes off again leaving them, and they don't seem of much importance to anybody. That was the way we felt, the pup and I—of not much importance to anybody—and the little Federal, he didn't have any opinion at that time. He didn't come around for some while, and we were glad when he did, the pup and I.

"The little Federal straightened himself out slowly, looked at the blood running across his hand and blinked at it. Then he saw me and the pup and smiled. I reckoned he thought it was all ridiculous, and I agreed with him there, but maybe he just meant to be polite. He certainly was polite.

"'What's up?' He asked; and I said there wasn't anything up; it was all down, and our luck was at the bottom. It made me mad to see him so cheerful when he hadn't any real excuse for it. But he smiled again and then closed his eyes.

"I judged he was faint, and that I ought to be doing something; so I crawled toward him, though it took a deal of grunting to drag a red-hot leg; and the sweat came out on my forehead.

"He opened his eyes and asked what was the matter.

"'Leg.'

"'To bad, old man,' he said, 'I'm sorry!'

"The shot was high up in his chest, and I didn't rightly know what lay around there inside. I didn't see much to do without water, and it was a good fifty feet over the rocks to the pool of the brook.

"'Water?' he said. 'That's so. I'm horrid thirsty. Are you? Why, you can't get down there, and I can't. But there are lots of ways to do things.'

"Then it struck me I'd heard Yankees were full of tricks, and forever inventing and figuring. So I kept quiet and watched the little Federal.

"He tried to sit up; it made him cough and struggle in his throat, but I helped him, and he propped himself against a stone. Then he fished in his pocket and pulled out about six hardtacks, which he laid on the ground and started fishing again. Hardtacks are common soldiers' rations, and they're nourishing, but you need blasting powder to eat them.

"I thought it was my turn and showed a canteen. That's a flat leather bottle. There was no water in that either, but it seemed to please him and he settled down to think about it, whistling and looking up to where the pine trees met overhead, and then down over the boulders to the glint of the pool just showing above them. He didn't seem to take to anything until he lit on the dog, and then he brightened up and chuckled. 'He isn't much to look at,' he said.

"That was an idea which had struck me, too. The pup was sort of dirty and grayish in color, and he slinked around when you looked at him as if he were embarrassed.

"'Wonder what's his name. Tommy! Hi!'

"The pup slinked around himself and whirled his tail in a manner that might be called excessive, seeming to signify that 'Tommy' was a good enough name for him, but probably he was only pleased to be recognized.

"'Tommy will do,' said the little Federal. 'Now then, you toss your canteen and see if he'll fetch it.'

"And Tommy didn't wait to be told. He went for that canteen like a lost brother. And then I saw the little Federal's idea; and you wouldn't think it, but while we were interested in the subject, there weren't any happier people in the state of Tennessee than the pup, the little Federal, and I. I lay back and laughed; it seemed amusing even to have a red-hot leg; the little Federal chuckled and coughed and choked, and the pup pranced around as if he expected Christmas all the year.

"I threw the canteen down by the boulders and Tommy brought it up. Then I took a long aim and scaled it over the top of them so that it fell in the pool, and Tommy went after it with enthusiasm and stayed some time.

"There was a black-headed kingfisher on a tree way up above, and he came down lower and appeared to be making comments on Tommy; but we didn't make out what they were, only we judged afterward he was calling Tommy two or three kinds of idiots. Then Tommy came back with the canteen wrong end up, and the water all run out, having taken it by the nearest end, which happened to be the bottom.

I am oppressed with a sense of the impropriety of uttering words on this occasion. If silence is ever golden, it must be here beside the graves of fifteen thousand men, whose lives were more significant than speech, and whose death was a poem, the music of which can never be sung. With words we make promises, plight faith, praise virtue. Promises may not be kept; plighted faith may be broken; and vaunted virtue be only the cunning mask of vice. We do not know one promise these men made, one pledge they gave, one word they spoke; but we do know they summed up and perfected, by one supreme act, the highest virtues of men and citizens. For love of country they accepted death, and thus resolved all doubts, and made immortal their patriotism and their virtue. For the noblest man that lives, there still remains a conflict. He must still withstand the assaults of time and fortune, must still be assailed with temptations, before which lofty natures have fallen; but with these the conflict ended, the victory was won, when death stamped on them the great seal of heroic character, and closed a record which years can never blot.
~ James A. Garfield at Arlington, Virginia 1868

"The little Federal said he was disappointed in that dog, but I told him we mustn't have family quarrels, and he said that was all right.

"At the next throw the canteen hit a boulder, but it bounced off into the water, and the pup brought it up sideways in his mouth and about half-full. So we allowed it was innocence and not malice that made him spill things.

"It was getting toward night and dusky in the gully. We moistened hardtacks and ate them; at least I did, and the little Federal some. But he was in bad shape, though he said nothing, and I could only wash off his wound and tie something over it. I didn't know what might be hit inside him, and I didn't like talking of it either, judging he wasn't good for long, by his fever and the choking in his throat.

"We neither of us brought up any very serious matters—nothing much even about the war, except that he wanted to argue Tommy was a Union dog, and I was ready to stand out he was Confederate—and I stand to it yet—it wasn't likely a dog of Union opinions would be loose in southern Tennessee; but we compromised, and allowed he might be neutral on account of his innocence.

"It seems strange that two alone in the night, in the midst of armies and likely about to die, should have nothing much to say, nothing of any importance. But I reckon we did some hard thinking. Tommy was like the little Federal in this, that while conversation was going on he kept his manners up to their level best and banged his tail cheerfully; but when nothing was being said he drooped and got low in his mind.

"It grew cold in the gully, and the stars came out in patches of sky between the pines; we got close together with the pup, rather shivery, between us.

"Oh, it was cold that night! Sometimes it makes one bitter and discontented with the world to think of such times, the pain and weariness of it all. But that won't do, and besides, it's no use. The little Federal, he had the right idea about it; he thought on the whole it paid to stay game.

"It was late in November—the twenty-fourth, I think. The sky was clear as glass; but the trees were mostly pine and spruce, which don't shed their leaves, and so made it dark in the gully—made it seem that there was only one cold and dark place in the world, the rest of it sparkling with stars; and that one place had been picked out and we dumped into it to get along as best we could. There wasn't much to do about it. It was a hard night, and we'll let it go at that.

"The morning came at last, light in the gully but not much warmth. Still there was no wind down there, though the trees were swinging and creaking above in the forest. The batteries began softly and far away, and we knew the battle was up once more. Once more, and how often after no one knew then.

"The little Federal's face looked peaked and hollow in the gray light, and showed what the night had been to him. I didn't like his looks.

"There were three hardtacks left, and the pup was persuaded to get more water. The little Federal didn't seem interested. He said, 'You'll eat 'em all, Johnny'; and I asked, 'Why?'

"'Well,' he said, 'I can't. Besides I'm going to peter out pretty soon, and they won't do me any good.'

"Somehow it seemed, then, that we had lived together a long time, the pup and the little Federal and I. The lumps came up in my throat and made me nervous, and I said, 'Don't you do it'; which, seeing he wasn't dying in the least because he wanted to, was idiotic enough; but he was that polite he didn't say so.

"'Shucks,' he said, 'I sha'n't make any fuss. I'm going easy. If you get a chance I'd be glad if you'd drop a line to my people; let 'em know how it was. Somebody'll be along by and by, and you and Tommy can whoop for 'em. And then you'll be a no-'count captive, Johnny, and go up north until properly exchanged, and hear yourself called a not-to-be-mentioned rebel; that's what you will.'

"And I knew all this was his way of saying he meant to stay game, and advising me to do similarly; though that isn't saying those predictions were not strictly correct, for it all happened to me after in precisely that way.

"I reckon maybe the little Federal wandered some that morning in his mind; and what he said, being sort of half-conscious, belonged to his private affairs, which we're not inquiring into now and were none of my business then. But I have one curious thing to mention, that he seemed to know accurately when his moment had come, which, I should judge, was an hour before noon.

"He opened his eyes, smiled at Tommy and me, and said something. I listened, and he said it again: 'I must go now. See you later, maybe.'

"And as near as I could make out he went right then.

"By and by, patches of sunlight dropped into the gully, and one moved across his face. It was an ordinary enough face, only I say it belonged to a very decent sort of a man and a gentleman altogether.

"Well, it was lonesome for Tommy and me. My broken leg began to get back on me in a hot fever, and it occurred to me maybe I'd go out of my head with the fever without letting his people know how it was. So I took the canteen and cut in the leather side of it, 'Billy Ames, 14th Mass.'

"But after a while that didn't seem enough, so I worked at it a bit more and cut, 'He was the right kind,' which I thought put things accurately enough in a general way.

"Then I didn't see any more I could do. I fell to having dreams and thinking I was somewhere else yet I heard through them all the sleepy sounds of the brook and the cannonading, and Tommy, lying beside me because he was sleepy too.

"It was late in the afternoon. Tommy began to yelp, and I made shift to sit up and shout, but I reckon it was only Tommy made any noise to speak of.

"There was trampling around and calling overhead, and at last they came down a distance up the gully—a Federal sergeant and some men detailed to look for wounded. They seemed to take things in and didn't ask questions, considering I was more or less wandering.

"But I recollect the sergeant reading, 'Billy Ames, 14th Mass. He was the right kind,' and saying he'd see the canteen through to Massachusetts; and I do recollect, too, how Tommy followed us out of the gully very low in his mind, with his tail between his legs, and nobody noticing him. I don't know where he went any more than where he came from, but I'll say for him that he was a well-meaning dog.

"And I recollect going down the mountain, carried somehow, but I don't remember how, and seeing in the distance the town of Chattanooga, and by it the shining loop of the river. And that was all."

Peggy McLean's mouth was wide open and astonished and sticky. "My!" she said, "weren't there any heroes?"

"Not this time, Peggy," said the colonel. "You can't have 'em all the time. We were three ordinary folks."

The Fallen by John Vance Cheney

Here in the warm May weather,
Bow we in grief together;
To them that fought so well,
To all that fought and fell,
Once more, farewell, farewell,
Once more, farewell.

Heroes of the Civil War
By Amy Puetz

Many brave men fought during the Civil War (or the War Between the States as it is sometimes called). See how many of them you know. Match the description on the left with the heroes on the right. Answers are below.

1. This general fought for the Confederacy. He was nicknamed "Stonewall" after standing his ground at the battle of First Manassas. In 1863 he was accidentally shot by his own men while he was behind enemy lines. His Christian faith comforted him before he died.
2. This Union general became the commander of the Union forces. He was nicknamed "Unconditional Surrender" after the battle at Fort Donelson where he said he would only accept unconditional surrender. After the war he served as the eighteenth president.
3. One of the most popular men of the South was this general who was the commander of the Army of Northern Virginia. He and his family lived at Arlington, a large estate his wife inherited from her father who was the grandson of Martha Washington.
4. This young Southern scout was captured by Northern troops and executed as a spy
5. A Northern drummer boy from Ohio won the admiration of his fellow soldiers when he shot a Confederate officer who was trying to block his return to the Northern line. This boy was called "The Drummer Boy of Chickamauga" after that.
6. This Northern man served as a major-general before being wounded. He later became the twentieth president and was the second president to be assassinated.

A. John Clem
B. General Thomas Jackson
C. General Robert E. Lee
D. Major-General Garfield
E. Samuel Davis
F. General Grant

Answers 1-B, 2-F, 3-C, 4-E, 5-A, 6-D

The Dead Volunteer by J. W. Barker

Silently, tearfully welcome the brave.
Glory encircles the patriot's grave.

Here let affection swell,
Here let the marble tell

How the brave hero fell,
Loving his country well.

Silently, tenderly, mournfully home,
Welcome the brave volunteers as they come.

Memorial Day

The Parshley Celebration

By Sarah Orne Jewett, 1899

Asa Binney's second wife was just the sort of tonic needed by the good people of Parshley. Everybody always said that there was no public spirit in the town of Parshley, and nobody ever seemed to think that it might be his own fault. When any great holiday or anniversary came, the fact was bewailed from house to house, and from field to field, that it was not likely "they" would do anything; they never did.

Asa Binney's second wife, a pleasant woman whom everybody liked, heard this familiar complaint one Sunday morning in May, just before Memorial Day. "Who do you mean by 'they'?" she asked eagerly.

Asa Binney himself and John Foster and three or four others who stood close by looked confounded by this unexpected question. Nobody answered until Mary Ann Winn, the complainer, broke an awkward silence.

"No, they never do anything to observe Memorial Day here," she repeated. "I never did see such a dead place as Parshley."

"There ain't much public spirit in Parshley now; it's very different from what it was when I was a boy," said old Mr. Storer with a kind of chivalry, as if he wished to uphold Mary Ann. All the listeners looked at Martha Binney with timid disapproval, but the brisk, good-hearted woman held her ground.

"What's the use o' talkin' about 'they'?" she asked pleasantly but with much spirit. "We've all of us, young an' old, got a way of throwin' the blame of such things on nobody in particular. I suppose if we wanted to celebrate we could do it just as well as anybody. We're 'they,' aren't we? We've got to do things ourselves if we want 'em done, in a little place like this."

By this time, the minister had come out of church and the rest of the congregation with him. It had been rainy in the early morning, and there were but few wagons tied to the fence, but Mrs. Binney was suddenly dismayed by the sight of a reproachful group of listeners.

"What great project is going forward now, Sister Binney?" asked the minister, and Asa came gallantly to his wife's assistance.

"We were speaking of Memorial Day, and feeling it ought to be noticed, Sir," he answered. "My wife was only saying we'd got to do it ourselves if it were going to be done. She ain't one that ever wants to throw the sermon over into the next pew!"

"All I said was that they never do observe the day; they ain't very public-spirited here in Parshley," insisted Mary Ann Winn, suddenly forsaking the attack and putting herself upon the defensive.

"And I asked who 'they' were; it sort of came home to me," said Mrs. Binney. "I was wonderin' if Sister Winn an' I could do anything ourselves."

Then everybody looked at the minister for an answer.

"I shall certainly give such a question my serious thought," said the Reverend Mr. Tasker, after a moment's reflection. "I shall do everything I can to help you," he added, with a smile of unaffected pleasure.

The worst now seemed to be over, and the company quickly separated, not without a sense of happy escape from an unexpected emergency.

There was no village at all in Parshley. It was one of the large townships of northern New England which sometimes get temporary notice through the public press by a statement that they have neither doctor nor lawyer nor public house within their boundaries; being made famous for what they are not and have not rather than for what they are and have. Such towns are often pleasant and prosperous in their own quietness, and if the truth were known, there is usually a doctor or a lawyer close at hand just over the border, in the next town.

As for Parshley, it had a post office of its own in John Foster's store near the church, and these two buildings, with the old Foster house and the minister's house, made a small group and neighborhood which had looked for many years as if it might grow to be a village in the course of time. The rest of the houses were thinly scattered. Almost every farm was like an island in a great tract of woodland or rough pasture. You could hardly look out of any window and see another light at night, but this was partly because the country was so nearly level.

John Foster and Asa Binney walked away together after church, leaving their wives to follow. It was a long drive to church from the Binney farm, and the younger couple were going to the Fosters' to dinner.

"Mary Ann Winn needn't have been so touchy," said Mrs. Foster, who was stout and already a little out of breath.

"Why, no!" exclaimed Martha Binney, with a pleasant smile. "I didn't mean to blame her, but you never get anything done in a place if you wait for it to do itself."

"What Mary Ann desired to say was that we don't seem to have any leaders nowadays. You've always got to have somebody to take the lead, you know," explained Mrs. Foster.

"Sometimes we've got to take hold and be leaders," answered Mrs. Binney. "I do think such timid persons as Miss Winn hinder others from acting free. They 'most make a credit o' hanging back!"

"There, there!" interrupted her companion, who was always a peacemaker, "when anything gets really started you'll find that Mary Ann'll work day an' night. She may not be one o' your leaders, but she's the best o' the other kind. She may wait for others to plan, but she'll never wait for others to do."

"That's a great point," acknowledged Mrs. Binney warmly, as they went in at the gate.

One day early in the week, Martha Binney finished her after dinner work in good season and changed her dress and sat down by the side window to her sewing. The spring was late and cold that year, but at last one could see a bloom of green on the fields. Asa Binney and his son and hired man were all busy out on the land with a piece of heavy, belated plowing. There was a clay side hill to be broken up, and every time the four-horse team came into sight over the ridge, Martha gave a quick, affectionate look at both horses and men.

The work was going on steadily. She had given the men an extra good dinner, and they had gone out to their long afternoon's drudgery in the best of spirits. She had only been married a year or two. Asa Binney's first wife had been an ailing, sad-hearted woman, who always hated farm-work and all that belonged to it, because she was neither strong enough nor able enough for a farmer's wife. Martha, who was large and vigorous and a good manager, took real pleasure in her hard work and good home.

"There, all I ever want is somebody to neighbor with," she said to herself. She had been used to village life before she married and was a very social person by nature.

The horses' heads came up again over the hill; she watched them strain at their collars, with the two young men running beside the half-broken, happy young leaders, and her husband came last, bending hard at his task of following the plow. They all stopped to rest and get their breath at the turn before they went along the slope. Asa was facing toward the house, and his wife smiled at him as if he were near enough to see.

"He's a good man," she said. "That's pretty stiff work for him. By the time Memorial Day comes he ought to have a spare day to rest."

As the team disappeared again, she slowly threaded her needle and put the big linen spool back on the worn window sill. Just then, in a lonely moment, she looked down the road and saw a figure approaching. Presently, she discovered that Mary Ann Winn was coming up the long footpath that shortened the way to the house across the field.

"Yes, that's Mary Ann, sure's can be," she said, with satisfaction. "I hoped 'twas Mis' Foster, but I might have known she couldn't walk so far. There, I'm well prepared as to supper, and Mary Ann always has plenty to say."

By this time the guest was near enough to the house to be saluted from the window, and Martha hastened to lay down her sewing and go to open the door.

"Now, you're going to take your things right off and stay and spend the afternoon, and ride home with Asa when he goes to the selectmen's meeting," she said heartily, and Mary Ann made but faint protest.

"Fortunately I happen to have my knitting in my pocket," she said, when she was comfortably settled in a high-backed rocking chair close to the window, where Mrs. Binney went on as before, mending an old coat. "The beautiful weather tempted me out. I didn't expect to get half as far as this when I started."

"I'm proper glad you came," answered the hostess. "I was just feeling lonesome. There's a time last o' the winter when the men folk don't have much to do outside and are right underfoot most all the time, but quick as they begin to be off all day, when spring opens, I do begin to miss 'em."

"That was just what Asa's mother used to say. I don't have no men folk the year 'round," said Mary Ann, in an inexpressive tone. "I 'most forget how 'twould feel now. Mother an' I lived alone 'most fifteen years, and it's seven now that I've had the house all to myself."

Martha Binney turned to look down the field, but the horses and men were not in sight; somehow, she could not look away until she saw them all coming.

"I was alone a good while after my mother died, too," she said softly. "I feel very contented now there's somebody to do for. Yes, I can understand your feelings, Miss Winn."

Mary Ann gave an unconscious sigh. "I expect Asa has told you that I was engaged to be married to his brother David," she said.

"Oh, yes indeed," said Martha, compassionately, "'twas dreadful hard for you, I'm sure."

"He was a handsome young man," said Mary Ann, "and 'twas a good while before I could bear to think of coming to the house here, but I love to come now. That daguerreotype in the front room that he had taken for his mother same time as mine don't do him any justice. I like mine the best, but they give hardly any idea of his looks. He was very tall and straight and carried his head high, just the picture of a soldier."

"Asa speaks of him a good deal; he feels his loss yet," said Martha; "'twas all the brother he ever had.'"

"Asa had to be the one to stay and carry on the farm," said Mary Ann Winn. "You know what a great farm it is, and his father wa'n't what he had been; the boys couldn't both go."

"Yes, 'twas a great disappointment," continued Martha. "Asa was telling me only Sunday night that he believed if he'd been there David wouldn't have died. He don't feel certain he had any sort of care."

"No, I don't either," said Mary Ann. She spoke in the same unconcerned voice, but the color came and went quickly in her thin cheeks. She turned and looked out of the other window across the room, and Martha looked, too. They could see two dark spruces on the ridge of land and a faded little flag that fluttered in the spring wind.

"As I was coming along, I couldn't help but think of what you said Sunday after meeting," Mary Ann said, frankly, after a silence. They both laid their work in their laps and looked eagerly at each other.

"We can't attempt any sort of a procession as they do in big places," she continued. "First place, there wouldn't be anybody to march. The soldiers' widows, and one or two more situated as I be, might all walk together and help out, but I don't know's 'twould be expedient. And I don't know either's we want to go to meeting and be preached to; we know all that can be said. I remember once the day came on Sunday and the Walton minister was here to exchange, and he gave an address on war matters in the afternoon, but it worked me up so I couldn't sleep all night. Scenes of the battlefield'll do to interest some o' the young folks. They don't know what war is."

Martha Binney looked up with tears in her kind eyes. "I think some of the women folk that stayed at home gave their lives to the country much as the men," she said.

"That year altered everything for me," said Mary Ann. "I've done the best I could; 'twas a great comfort to have Mother need me as she did. I've got sort of numb and used to things now, but I was dreadful full o' hope an' ambition when I was young. The day I saw David ride off in the wagon with Asa, going to the war, was the end of everything for me. He enlisted over to Walton."

"It does seem as if we ought to take some notice of Memorial Day," said Martha presently.

"Have you heard whether they're going to do anything this year?" asked Mary Ann with great eagerness, just as she had asked before, but somehow the words had a different sound to her listener's ears.

"Seems to me as if you an' I might overlook the ground and see if anybody stands in need of help. There isn't but a poor few of soldiers' families; we might just go an' see everybody that day and help those that need it and make a kind of friendly visit to the rest. 'Twould be a remembrance," said Martha Binney with shining eyes. "Asa was telling me Sunday night that he believed old Mis' Paterson on the East Road was having a hard time; he thought she wore a discouraged look, more so than usual. Her son died in hospital and left a young wife and family. They're grown up an' scattered, but he says none of 'em are doing much."

"'Tis a very poor farm an' always was, that Paterson farm," said Mary Ann. "Mis' Paterson's getting old; she's got no money to hire and needs help, both outdoors and in. I've been thinking lately I'd go over and make her a little visit and help along what I could, but 'tis quite a ways over there. Why, that's a beautiful idea to go 'round making calls. Anybody can do that!"

"Yes, we'll carry help to those that need it and make a friendly visit to the rest," repeated Martha, as if the plan were already settled to her satisfaction. "I want to make over some clothes for the little Ames boys; their grandma's a soldier's widow. I saw them in very poor array last Sunday."

"Eben Taft's the only veteran left in town now," said Miss Winn after much reflection. "He's well off, Eben is, and I know he'll take an interest."

"Asa an' I thought we'd speak with him tonight," said Martha Binney, disclosing her secret plan with final openness and generosity. And Mary Ann smiled as she had not smiled before in many a long day.

By twelve o'clock on Saturday, there were several small groups of persons scattered about the open space between Foster's store and the church, and when Asa Binney came driving up the road with his new hay rigging trimmed with green boughs and all his four horses decked with flags in their harness, everybody shouted and cheered.

There was not a wagon tied to the meeting house posts that did not carry a generous freight, and there were some carefully guarded baskets and bundles on the grass which belonged to the men and women who had come afoot. Asa Binney had provisioned the hay rigging as if it were going to put out to sea on a long cruise, and his wife and Mary Ann Winn had been sewing all the week with double diligence. They had followed the good Bible example of Dorcas, and now sat waiting like two queens in the long cart in two steady old kitchen chairs.

"Take those leaders by the head!" commanded Asa Binney, as his favorite young horses began to prance and rear, and all the boys within hearing rushed to obey.

"Oh, look!" cried Mary Ann Winn. "There's Eben Taft coming out of the store to go with us, and he's got on his uniform! I did so hope there would be something that looked like the soldiers!"

"Come along, Eben, you get right in and stand here 'long o' me," said Asa Binney, heartily, and the faded blue overcoat took its place at the front.

Then three or four others followed, men and women, including the minister and his wife and Mrs. Foster and last of all, John himself, who locked the store door after him. He brought a sheaf of flags under one arm and a large flag on a staff, which he gave to the old soldier.

"'Twas the best I could get," he said. "You ought to be the one to carry it, Eben."

"I've carried the colors before; I guess I can manage it," said Eben Taft proudly. "There, now we look complete; 'twas the one thing wanting. Start along now, Asa!"

The great cart moved heavily along the sandy road. It looked like a triumphal chariot, with its sober faces of men and women and the new flag flying at the front. One by one the country wagons all fell into line until there were ten in the procession, and a good many persons went afoot as far as old Mrs. Paterson's. On they went, slowly past the green May fields. It was the first day that seemed like summer, as if summer herself had come to this rustic celebration.

The tall, blue-coated figure of the veteran looked as soldierly as a whole regiment. This one aging man who had known all the glories, all the horrors of battle, was enough to remind every heart of an unforgotten war—enough to thrill the old with remembrance, and the young with a sudden waking of patriotism. This it was to love and serve your country and to wear her colors; this it was to be honored in a great day. Eben Taft had always come and gone humbly enough in their sight along the Parshley roads, but today he was a hero.

"Oh, yes, the folks have heard about our coming," said Martha Binney. "You see, 'twas most too big a secret to keep in a little place like this. Yes, there's Mis' Paterson standing right in her door, and dear heart if she ain't got a flag, too!"

To have such a procession stop at your door with laden hands, and eager, kind faces to be made of such consequence when you had long felt poor and dependent; to have it so nobly remembered that you were a soldier's wife or a soldier's mother, when this had only seemed to bring piteous disadvantage and forgetfulness in hard times, cheered more than one heart that lovely day. It seemed as if, having broken the long silence, nobody could do or say enough.

So the few soldiers' graves in the farm burying grounds were covered with spring flowers, and all the homely gifts from neighbor to neighbor were laid on the altar of patriotism. At every house they left a new, bright flag; at every stopping place they sang with all their hearts "My Country, 'Tis of Thee," or "Hail Columbia," or some old tune that everybody knew. And if it were a prosperous house instead of a poor one, still they left the flag, and sang, and lingered to speak of those who were gone, but this they did at all the houses that had sent men to the war.

"We came to see you today for John's sake," Eben Taft said to the old father and mother of one of his comrades. "I can tell you, for I know, that there wa'n't a braver fellow in the field than John, or one that was more neighbor like and kind all through that hard weather in winter camp."

And the old people standing side by side received this simple tribute gravely, but they began to cry when the minister led the singing.

"Sometimes it seemed as if everybody but us had forgot about our John," said the mother.

All the soldiers were counted again that day and remembered, and many a boy and girl wondered at the war stories that they had never heard before.

It was early evening; the cool, misty air was rising from the fields when the Binneys got home, and the young leaders of the four-horse team were well sobered down. Nobody was needed to take them by the head when they got back to their own green yard. The half-leaved maple boughs, which were mixed with pine on the cart trimming, were all wilted and dry, but the little flags were bright as ever.

Mary Ann Winn had come back to supper and to spend the night, for she and Martha had sat sewing and planning together for many days, and happily discovered themselves to be the best of friends. It was going to make a great difference in Mary Ann's life. They got down from the cart, still talking with eager excitement, and Asa handed their chairs after them.

"Just think of this being the first time we ever kept the day in Parshley," said Mary Ann. "How everybody joined right in, and it all went off so ready and easy! Parshley folks are very warmhearted underneath."

Martha Binney smiled. "Yes, we've had a beautiful day," she said.

"I shouldn't wonder if they did something now to celebrate the Fourth of July," said Mary Ann hopefully, but she could not quite understand why Mrs. Binney smiled again as she stood on the doorstep.

"Perhaps they will!" said Martha and then the two good, tired women went into the house together.

Memorial Day
By Amy Puetz

To honor those who have sacrificed their lives for us, decorate the grave of a soldier. Buy some red, white, and blue flowers or some small U.S. flags and go to their graves.

If you do not know a soldier take a few minutes to pray for the armed forced who defend the United States of America and for their families.

★★★★★ Memorial Day by Jane Campbell ★★★★★

Yes, scatter flowers above the graves
Where the Nation's dead are sleeping,
To tell that the comrades left behind
Their memories green are keeping.
'Tis many a year since they marched forth,
All the battle's perils braving,
And many a year above their graves
Has the long green grass been waving.

Yes, scatter the flowers, 'tis a kindly thought,
Pale lilies and fair red roses,
With lavish hands o'er the grave where each
Brave soldier in peace reposes.
Long years have passed since they sank to rest,
'Mid a nation's bitter mourning,
But their faithful comrades, year by year,
Bring flowers for their graves' adorning.

But far away upon hill and plain,
Nameless, forgotten, are lying,
The bones of many who bravely fought,
In their country's service dying.

But though their graves are unknown, unsought,
Our dear Lord covers them over
With the sweetest flowers and greenest grass,
And blossoms of scented clover.

And instead of the muffled beat of drums,
Its saddening memories bringing,
The only sound that the silence breaks
Is the note of some wild bird singing,
Or a rush of timid, rapid feet
As the wild gray rabbit passes,
Or the drowsy hum of the honeybee
As it flits among the grasses.

But peacefully still at rest they lie
And little it matters whether
Alone they sleep in their nameless graves
Or in churchyards close together.
For a grateful country in its heart
Is fresh their memories keeping.
So scatter flowers with a generous hand
Where the Nation's dead are sleeping.

Flag Day

June 14

On June 14, 1777, the Continental Congress issued the following proclamation:

Resolved, that the flag of the thirteen United States be thirteen stripes, alternate red and white; that the union be thirteen stars, white in a blue field, representing a new constellation.

Before this, the U.S. flag had many different designs, most of them were the flags of the states. Legend says that George Washington asked Betsy Ross of Philadelphia to sew the first flag.

In 1916 President Woodrow Wilson created a presidential proclamation making June 14, Flag Day. In 1949 President Harry Truman signed a law making June 14 a national holiday to commemorate the Stars and Stripes. Since that time, each president is supposed to issue a yearly presidential proclamation for Flag Day.

On Flag Day people proudly hang their flags to show their patriotism.

June 12

Our Flag's First Engagement

By H. A. Ogden, 1912

There is some debate among modern historians as to where the first U.S. flag was used, but this wonderful tale is believed by many to be the true story of the star spangled banner appearing in a military campaign. ~ Amy Puetz

ow many of our boys of today know where and when the star spangled banner was first raised, and that the honor belongs to New York state? How it was made, and under what circumstances, Tom Fosdick, a drummer boy of old Fort Stanwix, which stood near the site of the city of Rome, New York tells us.

"On August 3, 1777, the first day we were besieged, the need of a flag to fly from our bastions caused Colonel Gansevoort, our commander, to call me to him, saying, 'Tom, my boy, we must have a banner to fight under. I have, in a copy of the "Philadelphia Gazette," a full description of the new standard for the United States as ordered by the Congress in June, so hunt around and do your best to find something—anything, red, white, and blue—that can be sewn together and we'll show the enemy a banner that will tell them we are a new nation, with colors of our own. And a banner that we won't haul down, my lad, while there's one of us left to defend it.'"

"With this command, I rushed around, ransacking the barracks and storerooms, finally securing a couple of white ammunition shirts, and an old red cloth petticoat from the wife of one of our soldiers; but nothing blue could I find. Running back with my store of materials, I showed them to the colonel, telling him that I lacked the blue. Captain Swartout, standing nearby, said, 'I can furnish that,' and going to his quarters, quickly returned with a cloak of the right color, which he had captured at Peekskill. At once the stripes and field were cut, a paper pattern made for the stars, and in a short time our patchwork flag was put together. What mattered it if the red was somewhat faded in places, or that the seams were rough and uneven, the Stars and Stripes were there, and by sunset we were ready to unfurl our homemade standard to encourage us in our defense.

"Ezra James, my fellow drummer, and I beat the long roll, and at the word of command the sergeant pulled the halyards while, saluted by the officers and cheered by the garrison, up went our flag to the top of the staff. Ezra and I put our whole hearts into the beats we gave our drums, and never will I forget the delight I felt at seeing how brave and beautiful that 'first edition' of our nation's flag looked as the breeze caught its folds, whipping it out in graceful curves like a thing alive.

"Since early spring we had been hard at work trying to get the old fort, now called Fort Schuyler instead of Stanwix, into condition to withstand the enemy who were assembling at Montreal, and planning to capture us and then join General Burgoyne and his army at Albany. In July, Colonel Willett and his regiment had arrived as a reinforcement, so that now we mustered seven hundred and fifty, our commander being Colonel Peter Gansevoort of the New York Line Continentals. Our scouts, and some friendly Oneida Indians, brought tidings of the approach of Colonel St. Leger with a force more than double our own, of Regulars, Tories, and Indians—these last under the command of Brandt, the famous Chief of the Six Nations, lately made a captain in the British Army. Just before this foe arrived, a further reinforcement of two hundred men under Lieutenant-Colonel Mellon and two big flatboats laden with provisions and ammunition reached us, narrowly escaping the enemy's advance guard. Indeed, they cut off the captain in command and took him prisoner.

"The morning after our new flag was raised, there came a summons to surrender, which, of course, our commander promptly refused, and then the siege began in earnest. On the morning of August 8, messengers made their way to the fort from General Herkimer, who, with eight hundred men, was coming to our relief, three guns being a signal to him that they had reached the fort, but St. Leger, hearing also of our coming relief, detached a division of his Tories and Indians, to intercept Herkimer. This pause in the siege gave us a chance for the sortie that was part of General Herkimer's plan, which was to get the enemy between two fires. Our Colonel Willett now did a daring and courageous thing for, with two hundred and fifty men and one three-pounder cannon, he sallied out and furiously attacked the Tories' camp. Their commander did not even stop to put on his coat—he fled so quickly. The little force then stormed the Indians' quarters, and they, too, scattered into the nearby woods.

"Sending out from the fort seven wagons three times, they brought back loads of clothing, stores, provisions, and the commander's baggage and private papers. As most of the force that had left to intercept General Herkimer returned, we knew he must have been defeated. Indeed, on the following day, two officers, under a flag of truce, were sent to our sally-port, and being blindfolded, were taken to Colonel Gansevoort's quarters, the windows being close shuttered and candles lighted, and another summons to surrender was delivered.

"Among several of our officers, I crowded into a corner of the room, and heard one of the British officers say that Herkimer had been defeated and mortally wounded at Oriskany, that Burgoyne was in possession of Albany, and that if St. Leger's demands were not obeyed—well—he made quite a long speech of it, to which Colonel Willett replied by saying that Colonel Gansevoort had no idea of surrendering. So the messengers were sent back, and the siege was renewed with vigor.

"As the days went on and ran into weeks, our food and ammunition began to get scarce. Several of our men had been able to get through the lines with messages to General Schuyler, who was fighting Burgoyne near Saratoga. Other written demands to surrender were met with positive refusals, and then, as their cannon failed to break our ramparts, they tried to dig a mine under our strongest bastion.

"Fearing that they might starve us out unless we were reinforced, Colonel Willett and Lieutenant Stockwell volunteered to make their way to General Schuyler; so one dark, stormy night they started out. For nearly two weeks longer, the digging and firing was kept up, and then our stubborn commander assured us that unless help soon reached him, before our supplies were all gone, we would sally out at night and cut our way through their lines.

"It was late in the afternoon of August 22 that, while taking my turn at one of the fort guns, I saw a tremendous commotion in the camp opposite my position. Guns were being dragged away; men were running; tents abandoned, and I fairly yelled out to the colonel, who at the moment was below the rampart, 'They're running away! They're retreating!'

"What could it mean? We could see no force coming to our relief, nor hear any sounds of firing behind them, but there they were flying in every direction. At nightfall there came to the gate a ragged country boy, who, being taken at once to the colonel, told him how he had been sent out by General Arnold, who was marching to our aid, into the enemy's camp to frighten them with tales of a big army marching to take them in the rear. This boy, who had been condemned to be hung as a Tory spy, had been promised his freedom if he carried out this stratagem, an older brother being held in his stead to make sure that he would keep his promise. Joined by a couple of friendly Oneidas, they so frightened St. Leger's Indian allies that they decamped at once, in spite of all efforts to prevent them; and so the siege was raised, for, on the twenty-fifth, General Arnold's 'big' army of less than one thousand men arrived, followed the next day by that daring fighter himself.

"Most of our garrison went out after the fleeing enemy, but few of them could be found and brought back as prisoners. Knapsacks, guns, provisions, everything that could hinder flight had been thrown away, and all this had been caused by a clever ruse. Colonel Willett was left in command of the fort, and, with my regiment, I marched out with General Arnold to join our main army fighting Burgoyne, who had not, by any means, reached Albany, as we had been told. Our flag was still flying at the top of the staff on the old fort as we left. It had not been lowered during its first engagement."

Felt Flag Puzzle
By Amy Puetz

To make a flag out of felt, you will need four 9" x 12" felt sheets, one of red felt, one of blue, and two of white. Use a permanent marker to mark the lines on one of the white felt sheets for the red and white stripes, each $^{11}/_{16}$" high. Use the image at right as a guide. Mark the first stripe with an R and every other stripe with an R (see below).

Cut three long red stripes $^{11}/_{16}$ x 9 inches. Cut four short red stripes $^{11}/_{16}$ x $6^{10}/_{16}$ inches.

Cut the blue field 5¼ x 4¾ inches.

Cut the star out of white (use pattern at right).

Blue field 5¼" x 4¾"

$^{11}/_{16}$ x $6^{10}/_{16}$ inches

$^{11}/_{16}$ x $6^{10}/_{16}$ inches

$^{11}/_{16}$ x $6^{10}/_{16}$ inches

$^{11}/_{16}$ x 9 inches

$^{11}/_{16}$ x 9 inches

$^{11}/_{16}$ x 9 inches

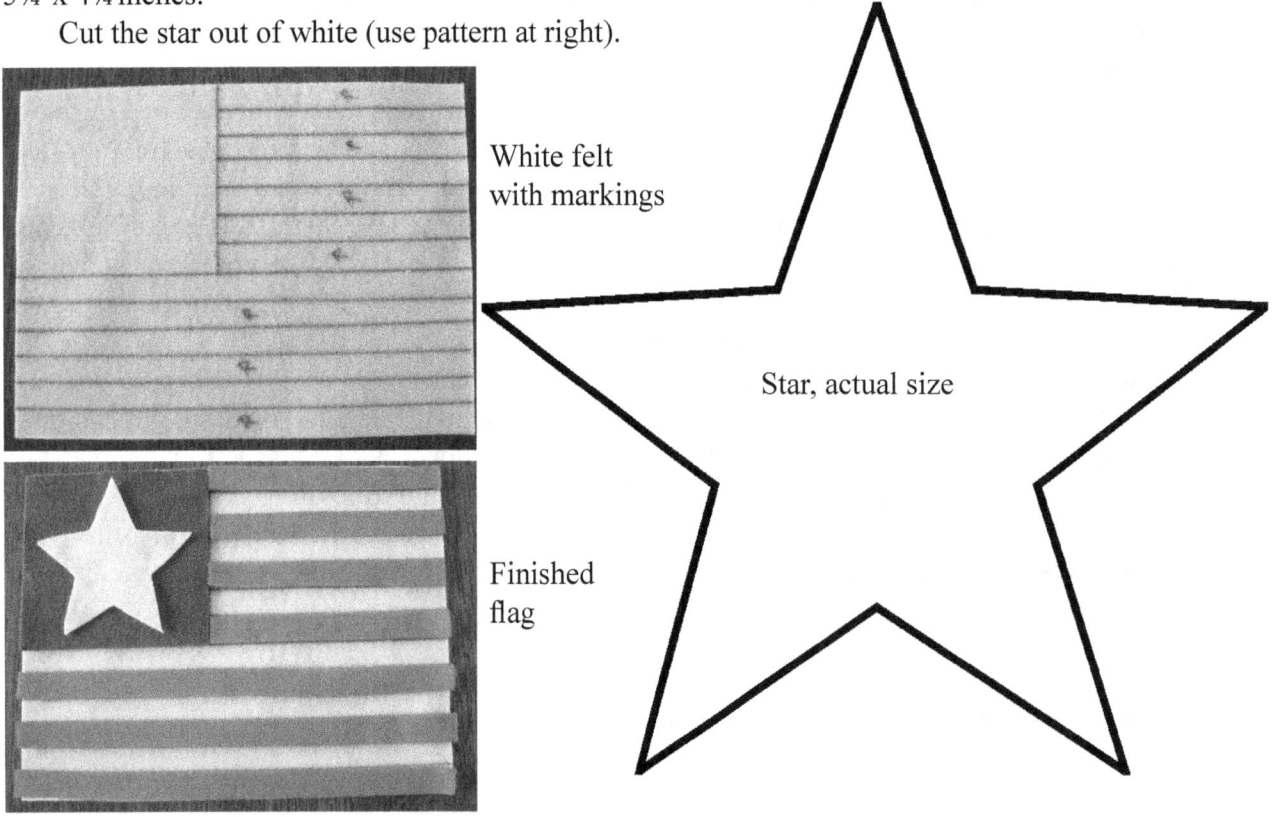

White felt with markings

Finished flag

Star, actual size

Summer Countdown   **Amy Puetz**

June 13

The Little Victory
By Dorothea Lay, 1921
Flag of Betsy Ross
By Harry Pringle Ford, 1914

The Little Victory
By Dorothea Lay, 1921

Six-year-old Bobby Downing ran out to the road and looked expectantly toward the village green. In the distance, he heard a faint thud, thud, thud. Bobby knew that sound well. For days the soldiers had been marching through the little town on their way to the fighting line in the South. Bobby ran up the road a little way, then stopped and watched the slowly moving line of men. As it disappeared, he turned and caught sight of his father coming down the road. He ran toward him, calling out happily, "Here comes Daddy. Daddy! Did you bring it? Did you bring it?"

"Yes, son, I have it. No, don't poke. I'll give it to you. Here it is. Now, run along and play."

Mr. Downing's voice was bright as he pulled out of his pocket the pretty little American flag and toy cannon, but his face was white, and for a second he grasped the child close to him.

Bobby was skipping down the road toward Rollie's house before you could say "Jack Robinson." Bobby found his friend, and as they had the afternoon's battles and parades all planned, they soon began work. First, they had a big parade and marched along the road to the place where Sister and Alice were waiting in a newly fixed-up hospital. Bobby used his harmonica and Rollie banged on the drum for music. Then finally, with a long-drawn-out note on the harmonica, the parade ended.

At last war began. Bobby and Rollie entered into the spirit of the fight with almost the intenseness of their older brother soldiers, and the two girl nurses ministered to their ghastly wounds and broken limbs with the care and gentleness they had so often seen used by their mothers at home. The battle was real to them, as real as that other great battle was to all people. They were excited, hot, and tired when Mother's startling call broke in on the fighting.

"Bobby, Bobby, come here. Bring Rollie with you."

The two boys had one last good firing, the little American flag still holding its place of distinction on Bobby's fort—and then they ran! Bobby grabbed his flag and cannon, but his legs were so short and his arms so chubby that the slender flag soon slipped out and landed stick first in the ground. There it waved gently on the dusty road.

★★★★★★★★★★★★★★★★★★★

A Song for Our Flag
by Margaret E. Sangster

A bit of color against the blue,
Hues of the morning: blue for true,
And red for the kindling light of flame,
And white for a nation's stainless fame.
Oh! Fling it forth to the winds afar,
With hope in its every shining star!
Under its folds, wherever found,
Thank God, we have freedom's holy ground!

Don't you love it, as out it floats
From the schoolhouse peak, and glad young throats
Sing of the banner that aye shall be
Symbol of honor and victory?
Don't you thrill when the marching feet
Of jubilant soldiers shake the street,
And the bugles shrill, and the trumpets call,
And the red, white, and blue is over us all?

★★★★★★★★★★★★★★★★★★★

All was excitement in Bobby's home that evening. The time had come. His father was called to the front! Mrs. Downing quietly moved to and fro arranging clothing, encouraging her husband, and seeing to the evening meal, while Bobby jumped about asking questions and trying to help.

Robert Downing slipped out of his house next morning and, with a farewell glance at his wife and children waving to him from the vine-covered doorway, turned abruptly down the road. As he turned the first curve, he suddenly spied something sticking out of the ground. He hastily bent over and picked up a dusty little cloth attached to a stick. There were the red and white stripes and the stars on the blue field. Old Glory! Bobby's flag! Turning for one more glance at his home, he tenderly folded it and laid it away in his pocket, then hastened on his way.

The worst heat of the summer hung over the battlefield, and one by one the men, fighting desperately, weakened and fell. Downing, still on the field unhurt, glanced about him. Despair seized him. So few men could never win—why should he go on? He fell back an instant as if to escape. Unexpectedly a picture of the last morning at home arose in his mind. He saw Bobby's flag waving in the dust; involuntarily, he put his hand in his pocket. There it was! For Bobby and his country, he must win! The next instant he was pushing forward, encouraging the man nearest him. That was what the flag meant. It encouraged men. It taught men to win, and it taught them to die fighting if winning was impossible.

With one hand clutching the little flag, Bobby's father staggered blindly on. Suddenly a piercing pain shot through his arm. Slowly he moved—and slower; then quietly he collapsed on the field.

A few hours later Bobby's father opened his eyes. Someone was bending over him. An agony of pain shot through his shoulder. The surgeon spoke, "Courage, man, we've won the battle, and we'll save you." Again all was darkness and depths. Minutes passed. Then slowly his eyes opened. His shoulder was quiet. He tried to move and stifled a moan. He stared straight ahead. Half consciously his eyes fell on the foot of his cot. Time passed and still he stared. There lay a battered, bloody remnant of Old Glory. He half perceived it and named it. "Little Victor" came through parched lips.

Flag of Betsy Ross
By Harry Pringle Ford, 1914

On the fourteenth day of June 1777, the Continental Congress passed the following resolution: "Resolved, that the flag of the thirteen United States be thirteen stripes alternate red and white; that the Union be thirteen stars, white in a blue field, representing a new constellation."

We are told that previous to this, in 1776, a committee was appointed to look after the matter, and together with General Washington they called at the house of Betsy Ross, 239 Arch Street, Philadelphia.

Betsy Ross was a young widow of twenty-four, heroically supporting herself by continuing the upholstery business of her late husband, young John Ross, a patriot who had died in the service of his country. Betsy was noted for her exquisite needlework and was engaged in the flag-making business.

The committee asked her if she thought she could make a flag from a design, a rough drawing of which General Washington showed her. She replied with hesitancy that she did not know whether she could or not, but would try. She noticed, however, that the star as drawn had six points, and informed the committee that the correct star had but five. They answered that as a great number of stars would be required, the more regular form with six points could be more easily made than one with five.

She responded in a practical way by deftly folding a scrap of fabric; then with a single clip of her scissors, she displayed a true, symmetrical, five-pointed star.

This decided the committee in her favor. A rough design was left for her use, but she was permitted to make a sample flag according to her own ideas of the arrangement of the stars and the proportions of the stripes and the general form of the whole.

Sometime after its completion it was presented to Congress, and the committee had the pleasure of informing Betsy Ross that her flag was accepted as the nation's standard.

Making a Five-Pointed Star
By H.B. Alexander, 1921

Take a square piece of paper or cloth and fold it in half; then fold it again so that it will resemble Fig. 1. Fold it again on the dotted line so that, when folded, it will be as in Fig. 2. Fold it over once more, again on the dotted line, when it should have the shape of Fig. 3. Then cut it as shown in the dotted line in Fig. 3, and you will have a symmetrical five-pointed star.

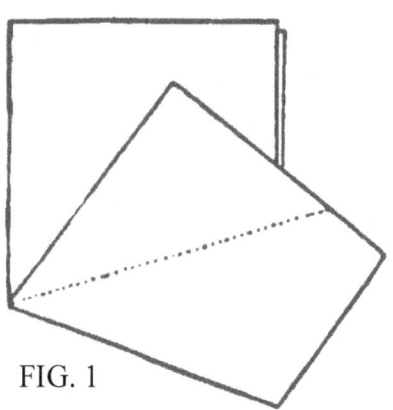

FIG. 1

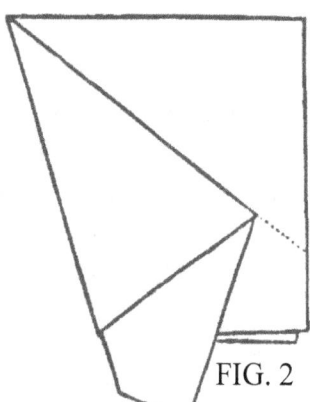

FIG. 2

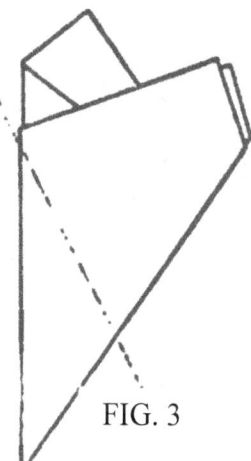

FIG. 3

Flag Day ~ June 14

Earning the Flag
By Carolyn Sherwin Bailey, 1918

"It's silk!" came in interested whispers from the corner of the assembly room where Five A sat.

"There isn't another flag like it in the Chestnut Street School," Five B declared. "Look at the cord and tassel and the golden eagle on top."

"The Chestnut Street kids will get it, of course; Chestnut Street first, and no chance for Long Pond," was the almost sullen murmur from the back of the room where the factory district boys and girls sat, not really belonging in the beautiful new brick school but transferred there for the term on account of crowded conditions in their own district.

But all the excited comments from the students were hushed as the principal of the school, Dr. Newton, rose and, standing by the beautiful Stars and Stripes on the platform, explained it.

"Flag Day is always a different day from any other patriotic holiday," he said. "It was celebrated first in our country to give us an extra chance to honor Old Glory. We should honor the flag in a special way this year by some kind of service to our country. The workmen from the factories have bought this flag for the boys and girls of this school. It is to be given to the class that shows the finest, largest kind of patriotism between now and Flag Day, June fourteenth. You have almost a month. Make it count. You are to choose and carry out your own kind of patriotism. The morning of Flag Day, we will meet here again and talk it all over and see who has earned the Stars and Stripes. Three cheers now for Old Glory!"

The hall echoed with them. Later, in the classroom, it was hard to settle down to problems in percentage and dates in ancient history. Wasn't history of today in the making right there before them in the silk folds of the flag, that each class felt sure it was going to earn? There was good reason too for their hopes. They talked them over in the yard at lunch.

"Thirty service flags; there's a flag with one star at least in the window of each of our houses," Jack Burden, the acknowledged leader of Five A, boasted proudly. "Some of our fathers or brothers or sisters are serving their country. If that doesn't beat the patriotism of Five B, I don't know what could. I guess the flag's ours right now, without any more bother."

It did seem as if it really were. No one spoke for a moment and then Marjory Blake touched Jack's sleeve gently. "I know that's a splendid showing, Jack," she said, "but our Junior Red Cross in Five B has a larger membership and has done more knitting than any other Junior Chapter in the county. It seems as if that ought to count. Don't you think that it may, Jack?"

Jack looked down kindly into the flushed, upturned face of his girlfriend and neighbor, Marjory. He wanted to encourage her, but he was anxious to see the new flag floating in his own classroom on Flag Day.

"Maybe so; Dr. Newton will decide, and—" Then he was interrupted. A flying figure, fists clinched, his cap worn awry, and his dark, tanned face still darker with anger, broke into the group of Chestnut Street boys and girls.

"They say over there in the corner of the yard that we can't even try for the American flag," the boy burst out. "They say we're not Americans, but I say we work for you. My father is an iron molder. He can bend iron to make an engine or the bow of a ship. He can stand the heat from a furnace door and not be afraid. He will work all night. I say we are Americans down at Long Pond!" The boy stopped, out of breath.

Jack put his hand on the lad's shoulder. He couldn't help liking this Russian boy, Boris, quick to fight, and as quick to shake hands again, with the folk stories of his home country at his tongue's end, and wits for his studies that all his mates envied. Still, he was in the wrong now.

"Cut it out, Boris," Jack advised, good-naturedly. "We know just how you feel about it, and, of course, you and Angelo and Dutchy and all the others from Long Pond will be Americans when you grow up and take out your papers, but you're not citizens yet. Don't feel bad about it, old man, but if I were in your place I wouldn't bother much about working for the flag. If it were one of your own flags or Angelo's now, it would be different, but—well, you see how it is—we're the Americans," he ended conclusively.

Boris's face paled a little, and his hands dropped at his sides. Jack was his hero in class work, games, and everything. He believed in him implicitly. Then he turned to the girl who was his friend also.

Marjory smiled kindly, but she shook her brown curls emphatically to show that she agreed with Jack.

"I think Jack's right, Boris," she said. "I'm awfully sorry, and if it were only you I wouldn't mind. But"—she glanced across the schoolyard at the motley crew of foreign boys and girls in old boots and bright shawls, now occupied in eating their various luncheons from the depths of red bandanna handkerchiefs— "you must see how it is, Boris. It's just got to be our flag. I don't know what you could do to get it."

Boris was silent. He couldn't understand, but he took his friends' word for it. He loved the Stars and Stripes. They had guided his steps down the gangplank of the great ship that had brought him and his mother and father to this wonderful land of the free. The flag flew over the schoolhouse where he was learning the things that only the rich boys in his own country were privileged to learn. And there was the little cottage down at Long Pond, with its pocket-size garden, and a boat on the water, and no landholder to come and collect tithes. It was under the shadow of the great factory whose shrill whistle was a kind of trumpet call to Boris every day. The factory's huge masses of black smoke twisting up to the blue sky seemed to the boy like the genie of a fairy tale, pointing the track that great aircraft would take, propelled by the engines his father helped to make. But he wasn't an American, and he couldn't try to earn the flag for his class. Boris turned quickly and dropped his head. He didn't want Jack to see the tears that had welled themselves into his eyes.

Those were busy days that followed. Jack and the others in his class made out a careful record of the absent ones in service for the colors from each of the Five A homes. It was a splendid showing—Army, Navy, Red Cross, medical, one chaplain, and many YMCA workers. Marjory's class Chapter of the Junior Red Cross had a fair that brought in quite a sum for the treasury, and then arranged some tableaux to give the afternoon before Flag Day. Other classes wrote compositions on town history, made current event scrapbooks, and learned patriotic recitations to give in honor of the Stars and Stripes. The long blue days of May and the beginning of June were happily full of these preparations. Trees burst into green, lawns were dotted with tulips and daffodils, and rose bushes budded. The earth seemed very good indeed and peaceful, in spite of daily war news. Then the unexpected happened. The Long Pond factory men went out on strike.

No one had realized, until Waterford's quiet, tree-lined Main Street overflowed with the Pond's foreign element, how large a settlement had sprung up, in the mushroom-like cottages about the aircraft factory. The dark, soot-begrimed workmen, sullen and defiant, walked the streets all day and gathered in threatening groups at the corners at night.

"They don't seem to know what they want," Jack said to Marjory on the morning of Flag Day. He had stopped at her house to take her to school, for her mother thought the streets were too unsafe for her alone. "Father said they had a meeting in the town hall last night, and an engineer from the government was there, telling them all about what wonderful things American airplanes are going to do for our country, and how the men are keeping it all back by stopping work. Boris' father is a kind of leader of the factory men, and Boris was there with his mother. But the men wouldn't listen to the engineer; they just hissed at him and walked out."

"Well, one trouble, I think, is that they don't understand English well enough," Marjory said wisely. "Now, if they were only all like Boris—"

"Oh, Boris!" Jack commented as if the lad's name alone spelled understanding. "Here we are," he went on as they turned in at the school door, "and we'll find out if it's your class or mine that gets Old Glory!"

There was a hush over the Flag Day Assembly. Everyone felt that the town's patriotism had been hurt by the walkout at the factory. "America" and "The Star Spangled Banner" seemed somehow to be sung less heartily, and there were big gaps in the Long Pond places. Many of the boys and girls were absent or straggled in late and looking sullen. Boris was noticeably absent.

The opening exercises were about over when there was a stir at the back of the room. The door opened, and a dark-browed giant of a man came in and walked down the aisle to the platform. He was followed by Boris, flushed with embarrassment.

"Boris' father," Jack whispered to a friend. "He looks like the giant smith, Vulcan, doesn't he?"

The Russian spoke in broken English to Dr. Newton, who looked first surprised, and then amazed. As the man started to go, Dr. Newton detained him and Boris also. He spoke to the assembly.

"Boris' father came to explain why he is tardy," he said. "It is for such an unusual reason that I want Boris himself to tell his mates of our Chestnut Street School. Tell them, lad. Don't be afraid," Dr. Newton said.

Boris hesitated, drew a quick breath, and then began speaking, his clear voice reaching to the very end of the room.

"It was about the strike at the factory," Boris said. "My mother and I went to a meeting about it, and I listened to what an American said about needing my father's work at the factory. 'A great factory,' he said, 'and a great American citizen would work in it for his country without striking, and the czar of this country would see that he was treated fair.' So I talked it over with my father afterward and told him that this was how he could be an American, and I too. I told Angelo to tell his father, and Dutchy his. We went to all the Long Pond boys this morning, and they asked their fathers to be Americans and go back to work in the factory. My father goes now to his work with the others," Boris finished simply.

As the children looked at Boris and his father, the latter standing there with his sleeves rolled up so that the great knotted sinews in his arms showed, it seemed to them that a great moving picture were unfolding itself before them. Under the Stars and Stripes marched the soldiers who defended it, and the sailors, but following them came the laborers, strangers in our land, but molders of metal and pounders of rock, giving the nation transportation and roads, and tilling the soil to provide food for the country. It seemed the most natural thing in the world for Dr. Newton to put the prize flag into Boris' arms, where its folds touched his father too. The room was one great voice with the cheers of the boys and girls, and when they grew quiet, Dr. Newton spoke again.

"I wish that we had a flag for each class that has done so much to deserve it," he said, "but Boris has done something for his country without any thought of reward, and it is a very great achievement."

"Hurrah for Boris!" they began again.

"Boris—American!" Jack's voice could be heard shrilly above the others.

The Star Spangled Banner

This song was written in 1814 during the War of 1812. Francis Scott Key watched the bombardment of Fort McHenry. After the battle, he saw Old Glory still flying, and he wrote this song. Sing this song.

The Star Spangled Banner

Summer Countdown   Amy Puetz

Father's Day
Third Sunday in June

A lady sat quietly during a Mother's Day sermon! The minister spoke of the tender heart a mother has. Sonora Louise Smart Dodd agreed, but she also thought of the wonderful influence a father has. Sonora's mother had died while she was a child and her father raised her and her five siblings. William Jack Smart had served during the Civil War and deeply loved his children.

"Surely a day should be set aside to honor fathers too," Sonora thought. Since her father's birthday was in June she encouraged local churches in Spokane, Washington to celebrate Father's Day during that month. In 1910 the first Father's Day celebration took place in Spokane.

From these humble beginnings, the special day was on its way to becoming a national holiday. In 1924 President Calvin Coolidge made it a national event to "establish more intimate relations between fathers and their children and to impress upon fathers the full measure of their obligations."

Father's Day became an official holiday in 1966 when President Lyndon Johnson proclaimed the third Sunday in June to be Father's Day. In 1972 President Richard Nixon signed it into law.

Friday before Father's Day

How the Home was Built

By Maud Lindsay, 1912

Once there was a very dear family—Father, Mother, big brother Tom, little sister Polly, and the baby, who had a very long name, Gustavus Adolphus—and everyone of the family wanted a home more than anything else in the world.

They lived in a house, of course, but that was rented; and they wanted a home of their very own, with a sunny room for Mother and Father and Baby, with a wee room close by for the little sister; a big, airy room for brother Tom; a cozy room for the cooking and eating; and, best of all, a room that Grandmother might call her own when she came to see them.

A box which Tom had made always stood on Mother's mantel, and they called it the " Home Bank," because every penny that could be spared was dropped in there for the building of the home.

This box had been full once and was emptied to buy a little piece of ground where the home could be built when the box was full again.

The box filled very slowly, though, and Gustavus Adolphus was nearly three years old when one day the father came in with a beaming face and called the family to him.

Mother left her baking, and Tom came in from his work; and after Polly had brought the baby, the father asked them very solemnly: "Now, what do we all want more than anything else in the world?"

"A home!" said Mother and brother Tom.

"A home!" said little sister Polly.

"Home!" said the baby, Gustavus Adolphus, because his mother had said it.

"Well," said the father, "I think we shall have our home if each one of us will help. I must go away to the great forest, where the trees grow so tall and fine. All winter long I must chop the trees down, and in the spring I shall be paid in lumber, which will help in the building of the home. While I am away, Mother will have to fill my place and her own too, for she will have to go to market, buy the coal, keep the pantry full, and pay the bills, as well as cook and wash and sew, take care of the children, and keep a brave heart until I come back again."

The mother was willing to do all this and more, too, for the dear home, and brother Tom asked eagerly, "What can I do? What can I do?" for he wanted to begin work right then, without waiting a moment.

"I have found you a place in the carpenter's shop where I work," answered the father. "And you will work for him, and all the while be learning to saw and hammer and plane, so that you will be ready in the spring to help build the home."

Now, this pleased Tom so much that he threw his cap in the air and shouted, which made the baby laugh; but little Polly did not laugh, because she was afraid that she was too small to help. But after a while the father said: "I shall be away in the great forest cutting down the trees; Mother will be washing and sewing and baking; Tom will be at work in the carpenter's shop; and who will take care of the baby?"

"I will, I will!" cried Polly, running to kiss the baby. "And the baby can be good and sweet!"

So it was all arranged that they would have their dear little home, which would belong to everyone, because each one would help, and the father made haste to prepare for the winter. He stored away the firewood and put up the stoves, and when the woodchoppers went to the great forest, he was ready to go with them.

Out in the forest, the trees were waiting. Nobody knew how many years they had waited there, growing every year stronger and more beautiful for the work they had to do. Everyone of them had grown from a baby tree to a giant; and when the choppers came, there stood the giant trees, so bare and still in the wintry weather that the sound of the axes rang from one end of the woods to the other. From sunrise to sunset the men worked steadily, and although it was lonely in the woods when the snow lay white on the ground, and the cold wind blew, the father kept his heart cheery. At night, when the men sat about the fire in their great log house, he would tell them about the mother and children who were working with him for a home.

Nobody's ax was sharper than his or felled so many trees, and nobody was happier when springtime came and the logs were hauled down to the river.

The river had been waiting too, through all the winter, under its shield of ice, but now that spring had come, and the snows were melting, and all the little mountain streams were tumbling down to help, the river grew very broad and strong, and dashed along, snatching the logs when the men pushed them in and carrying them on with a rush and a roar.

The men followed close along the bank of the river, to watch the logs and keep them moving; but at last there came a time when the logs would not move but lay in a jam from shore to shore while the water foamed about them.

"Who will go out to break the jam?" said the men. They knew that only a brave man and a nimble man could go, for there was danger that the logs might crush him and the river sweep him away.

They looked at each other. But the father was not afraid, and he was surefooted and nimble; so he sprang out in a moment, with his ax, and began to cut away at the logs.

"Some of these logs may help to build a home," he said, and he found the very log that was holding the others tight, and as soon as that was loosened, the logs began to move.

"Jump! Jump!" cried the men as they ran for their lives; and, just as the logs dashed on, with a rumble and a jumble and a jar that sent some of the logs flying up in the air, the father reached the bank safely.

The hard work was over now. After the logs had rested in the log "boom," they went on their way to the sawmills where they were sawed into lumber to build houses, and then the father hurried home.

When he came there, he found that the mother had baked and washed and sewed and taken care of the children, as only such a precious mother could have done. Brother Tom had worked so well in the carpenter's shop that he knew how to hammer and plane and saw and had grown as tall and as stout as a young pine tree. Sister Polly had taken such care of the baby that he looked as sweet and clean and happy as a rose in a garden, and the baby had been so good, that he was a joy to the whole family.

"I must get this dear family into their home," said the father; and he and brother Tom went to work with a will. And the home was built with a sunny room for Father and Mother and Baby, a wee little room close by for good sister Polly, a big airy room for big brother Tom, a cozy room for the cooking and eating, and best of all, a room for the dear Grandmother, who came then to live with them all the time.

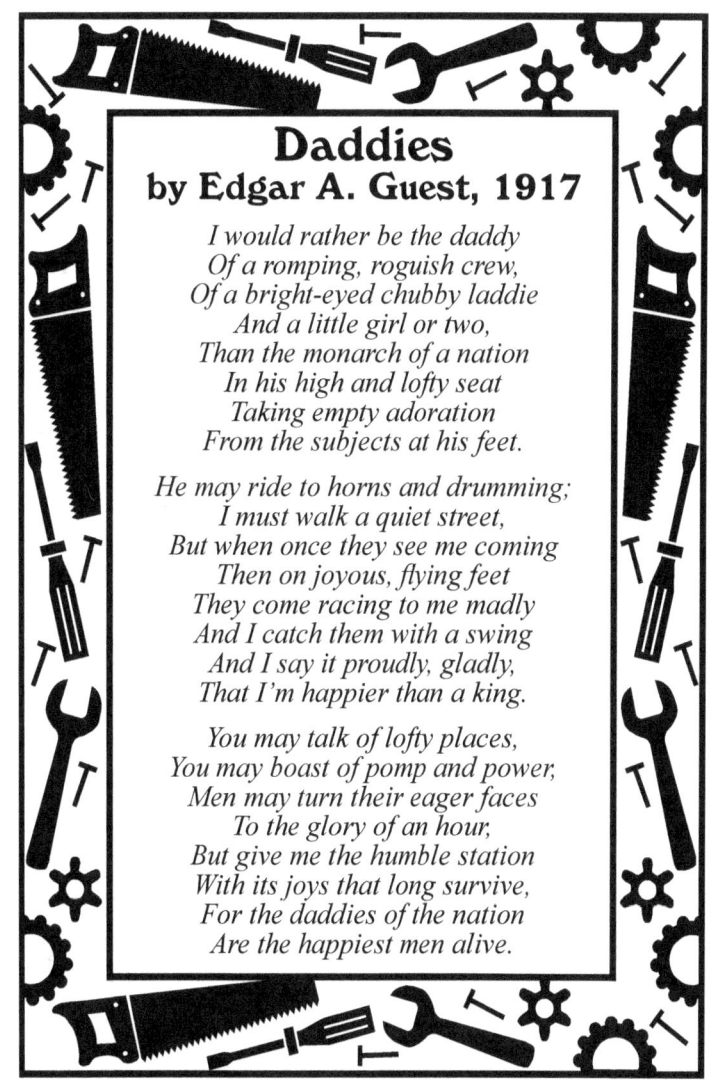

Daddies
by Edgar A. Guest, 1917

*I would rather be the daddy
Of a romping, roguish crew,
Of a bright-eyed chubby laddie
And a little girl or two,
Than the monarch of a nation
In his high and lofty seat
Taking empty adoration
From the subjects at his feet.*

*He may ride to horns and drumming;
I must walk a quiet street,
But when once they see me coming
Then on joyous, flying feet
They come racing to me madly
And I catch them with a swing
And I say it proudly, gladly,
That I'm happier than a king.*

*You may talk of lofty places,
You may boast of pomp and power,
Men may turn their eager faces
To the glory of an hour,
But give me the humble station
With its joys that long survive,
For the daddies of the nation
Are the happiest men alive.*

Make a Father's Day Card

Copy this page and color it. Fold an 8½ by 11 sheet of colored card stock in half and glue the colored picture to it. Write a nice note inside the card and sign it. Give it to your father on Sunday.

Saturday before Father's Day

The Story of William Tell
By James Hiram Fassett, 1914
Letter to His Son
By Theodore Roosevelt, 1905

The Story of William Tell
By James Hiram Fassett, 1914

Many years ago, high up among the steep mountains of far-off Switzerland, lived a man named William Tell.

Tell was a brave man and a great hunter, and he was the best shot with the crossbow in all the land.

At that time, his country was ruled by a wicked man named Gessler. Gessler liked to show his power and made many harsh laws which the people had to obey.

He even placed his hat on a tall pole and ordered that everyone who passed should bow to the hat.

Now these brave people hated the thought of bowing to a hat, and not one of them would walk by the place where the pole was set up. Thus, no one ever bowed to the hat, because no one ever passed it.

It happened that William Tell, who lived among the high mountains, had not heard about this strange law of bowing to the ruler's hat.

One morning he came into the village, leading his little son by the hand. He was walking straight past the hat, when the soldier who was always on guard shouted, "Halt! Why do you not bow before the hat of your master?"

"Why should I bow before a hat?" asked Tell.

"That hat belongs to Gessler, your ruler. He orders you to bow before it."

"I care not who orders it. I will never bow before a hat," said Tell quickly.

"Then you must come with me to prison," commanded the soldier.

"I will neither bow to the hat nor be taken to prison," and stepping back, Tell grasped an arrow for his crossbow.

Just then, Gessler rode up with a company of soldiers.

"What is all this noise about?" he asked.

"This man, William Tell, will not bow to your hat," said a soldier.

"So you are Tell," said Gessler, riding up close to him. "They say you are the finest shot with the crossbow in the land. Tell me, my man, is it true?"

"I have shot against many good men," replied Tell modestly.

"I have a mind to try your skill," said Gessler, "and I promise you, if you can hit the mark I offer, you shall go free."

"I shall be glad to shoot for you," said Tell. "Where is your mark?"

"Is this your son?" asked Gessler, pointing to the boy.

"Yes."

"Is he a brave lad?"

"I think he is."

"Then he can help you. Let the lad stand in front of that great oak. Place this apple on his head. If, with one arrow, you can hit the apple, then you shall go free."

The cruel man smiled as he spoke these words. Even his own soldiers were filled with horror.

"Would you ask me to shoot at my own boy?" cried Tell. "I will not do it."

But the boy was not afraid, and looking into his father's face, he said, "Father, I will stand straight and still. You never miss your mark. I know you can hit the apple."

The brave lad reached up and took it from Gessler's hand. Then walking to the tree, he placed the apple carefully on his head. "Now, father," he said, "I am ready."

Tell, looking over his quiver, picked two long, straight arrows. One he placed in his belt, the other he slowly fitted to his crossbow. Taking careful aim, he loosed the string.

The arrow flew straight to the mark. The apple fell, shot through the center, and the boy ran to his father, who took him in his strong arms.

Gessler turned to William Tell. "Why did you place the second arrow in your belt?" he asked. "Tell me, and you shall come to no harm."

Tell looked into the eyes of Gessler and said, "The second arrow was for your heart, had the first one harmed even a hair of my boy's head."

Gessler shook with fear at these bold words. Turning to his soldiers, he said, "Seize this man and take him to the strongest cell in my castle across the lake."

Before Tell could move, the soldiers seized him and bore him to a boat on the shore of the lake. As they were rowing across the water, a great storm arose. The waves dashed against the boat. Adding to the danger, darkness fell upon the water, and the men could not tell which way to row.

At length the soldier in command turned to William Tell and said, "You are a sailor and know this lake better than we do. If we untie your hands, will you help to save the boat?"

"I will," said Tell.

Then they cut the ropes that bound him, and as soon as he was free, Tell took charge of the steering oar. Knowing the lake well, he soon brought the boat close to a little point of land.

Before they could stop him, Tell seized his crossbow, and as he jumped to the shore, he gave the boat a great push out into the lake.

"Seize him! Kill him!" shouted the leader, but he was too late. Tell had already hidden himself in the bushes which fringed the shore.

It did not take him long to climb to his mountain home, where he was free from the power of the wicked Gessler.

Not long afterward the whole nation went to war against their enemy. Gessler was killed, and in the end the brave people, led by William Tell, became free.

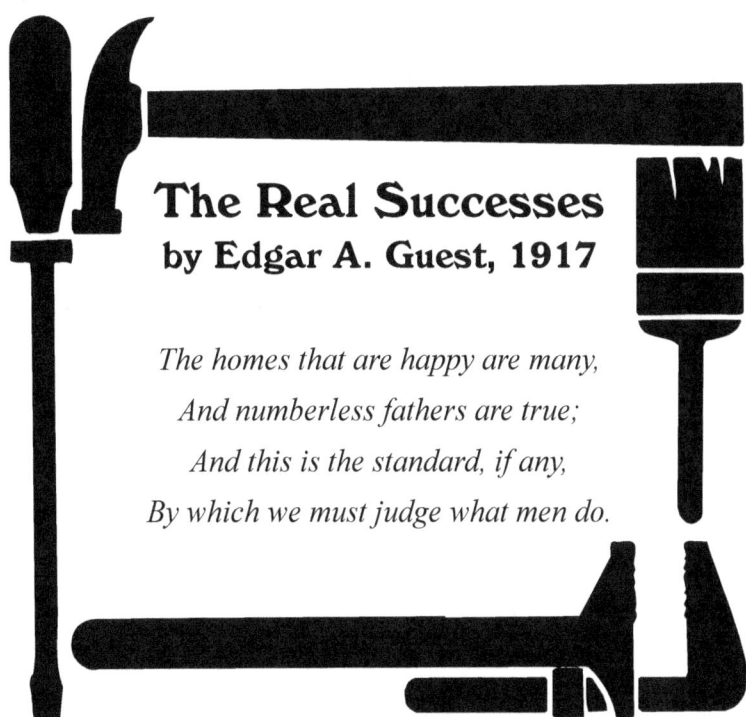

The Real Successes
by Edgar A. Guest, 1917

The homes that are happy are many,
And numberless fathers are true;
And this is the standard, if any,
By which we must judge what men do.

Letter to His Son
By Theodore Roosevelt, 1905

White House, November 19, 1905.

Dear Kermit,

I sympathize with every word you say in your letter, about *Nicholas Nickleby*, and about novels generally. Normally I only care for a novel if the ending is good, and I quite agree with you that if the hero has to die he ought to die worthily and nobly, so that our sorrow at the tragedy shall be tempered with the joy and pride one always feels when a man does his duty well and bravely. There is quite enough sorrow and shame and suffering and baseness in real life, and there is no need for meeting it unnecessarily in fiction. As Police Commissioner it was my duty to deal with all kinds of squalid misery and hideous and unspeakable infamy, and I should have been worse than a coward if I had shrunk from doing what was necessary; but there would have been no use whatever in my reading novels detailing all this misery and squalor and crime, or at least in reading them as a steady thing. Now and then there is a powerful but sad story which really is interesting and which really does good; but normally the books which do good and the books which healthy people find interesting are those which are not in the least of the sugar-candy variety, but which, while portraying foulness and suffering when they must be portrayed, yet have a joyous as well as a noble side.

THEODORE III, ARCHIBALD, THEODORE II, QUENTIN, & KERMIT IN 1907

We have had a very mild and open fall. I have played tennis a good deal, the French Ambassador being now quite a steady playmate, as he and I play about alike, and I have ridden with Mother a great deal. Last Monday when Mother had gone to New York, I had Selous, the great African hunter, to spend the day and night. He is a perfect old dear, just as simple and natural as can be and very interesting. I took him (with Bob Bacon, Gifford Pinchot, Ambassador Meyer, and Jim Garfield) for a good scramble and climb in the afternoon, and they all came to dinner afterward. Before we came down to dinner, I got him to spend three-quarters of an hour in telling delightfully exciting lion and hyena stories to Ethel, Archie, and Quentin. He told them most vividly and so enthralled the little boys that the next evening I had to tell them a large number myself.

Today is Quentin's birthday, and he loved his gifts, perhaps most of all the weest, cunningest live pig you ever saw, presented him by Straus. Phil Stewart and his wife and boy, Wolcott (who is Archie's age), spent a couple of nights here. One afternoon we had hide-and-go-seek, bringing down Mr. Garfield and the Garfield boys, and Archie turning up with the entire football team, who took a day off for the special purpose. We had obstacle races, hide-and-go-seek, blind-man's bluff, and everything else, and there were times when I felt that there was a perfect shoal of small boys bursting in every direction up and down stairs, and through and over every conceivable object.

Mother and I still walk around the grounds every day after breakfast. The gardens, of course, are very, very disheveled now, the snapdragons holding out better than any other flowers.

Activities for Father's Day

The games mentioned in the Mother's Day section might be adapted to fathers.

See how well you know your father. Fill in the information below and then ask your father the questions to see if you answered them correctly.

Father's Favorites

What is your favorite food?
___

What is your favorite snack?
___

What is your favorite dessert?
___

What is your favorite color?
___

What is your favorite place to visit?
___

Who is your favorite person in history?
___

What profession did you want to have when you were a child?
___

What is your favorite car?
___

What is your favorite animal?
___

What is your favorite pastime?
___

What is your favorite sport and who is your favorite sports team?
___

Father's Day

The Prodigal Son
Retold by Jesse Lyman Hurlbut, 1904

The Wise Father
By Ernest Clark Hartwell, 1921

The Prodigal Son
Retold by Jesse Lyman Hurlbut, 1904

A certain man had two sons. The younger of his sons said to his father, "Father, give to me the share that will come to me of what you own."

Then the father divided all that he had between his two sons. Not many days after, the younger son took his share and went away into a far country, and there he wasted it all in wild and wicked living. When he had spent all, there arose a mighty famine of food in that country, and he began to be in want.

He went to work for one of the men in that land, and this man sent him into the fields to feed his hogs. The young man was so hungry that he would have filled himself with the husks that were fed to the hogs, but no one gave anything to him. At last the young man began to think of his father's house, and he said to himself, "How many hired servants of my father's have bread enough and to spare while I am dying here with hunger! I will arise and will go to my father and will say to him, 'Father, I have sinned against heaven and in your sight. I am no more worthy to be called your son. Let me be one of your hired servants.'"

And he rose up to go back to his father's house. But while he was yet afar off, his father saw him and ran and embraced him and kissed him.

And the son said unto him, "Father, I have sinned against heaven and in your sight. I am no more worthy to be called your son—"

But before he could say any more, his father called to the servants and said, "Bring out quickly the best robe and put it on him. Put a ring on his hand and shoes on his feet, and bring the fatted calf and kill it. Let us eat and make merry for my son was dead and is alive again. He was lost and is found."

Now his elder son was in the field, and as he came and drew near to the house, he heard music and dancing. And he called to him one of the servants, and asked what these things might be. And the servant said to him, "Your brother has come, and your father has killed the fatted calf and is having a feast because he is at home safe and sound."

But the elder brother was angry and would not go in, so his father came out and urged him. But he answered his father and said, "I have served you for these many years; and I have never disobeyed your commands, yet you never gave me even a young lamb that I might make merry with my friends. But when this your son has come, who has wasted your money with wicked people, you killed for him the fatted calf!"

And the father said to him, "My son, you are always with me, and all that I have is yours. But it was fitting that we should make merry and be glad, for this your brother was dead and is alive again. He was lost and is found."

"Blessed indeed is the man who hears many gentle voices call him father."

~Lydia Maria Francis Child

The Wise Father
By Ernest Clark Hartwell, 1921

In Persia there once lived a wealthy merchant who was known all over the world for his wisdom and generosity. One day, when he had become a very old man, he called his three sons together and said to them, "My sons, I have lived long and have scarcely known a day of leisure, so busy have I been in heaping up wealth. Now, here are my possessions. They are yours. I have divided them into three equal parts, and to each of you I give a part.

"But there is one thing that I cannot give you, for it is very precious and cannot be divided. It is this diamond ring—the most costly of all my possessions. I will give it to that one of you who does the noblest deed. Go, each of you, and travel for six months. Then return and tell what you have done."

So the sons departed. They traveled in different directions, and at the end of the time, all returned to tell what they had seen and done.

The eldest son spoke first and said, "On my journey a stranger asked me to guard a large number of valuable jewels. I could easily and safely have taken some of them and made myself rich. But I gave the package back to him exactly as I received it. Now, wasn't that a noble deed?"

The father answered, "To be simply honest is not to be noble. You did only what is right. You acted well but not nobly."

The second son said, "One day I saw a child, who was playing on the bank of a deep river, fall into the water. I jumped from my horse and leaped into the water, and after

The Man to Be
by Edgar A. Guest, 1923

Some day the world will need a man of courage in a time of doubt,
And somewhere, as a little boy, that future hero plays about.
Within some humble home, no doubt, that instrument of greater things
Now climbs upon his father's knee or to his mother's garments clings.
And when shall come that call for him to render service that is fine,
He that shall do God's mission here may be your little boy or mine.

Long years of preparation mark the pathway for the splendid souls,
And generations live and die and seem no nearer to their goals,
And yet the purpose of it all, the fleeting pleasure and the woe,
The laughter and the grief of life that all who come to earth must know
May be to pave the way for one—one man to serve the Will Divine
And it is possible that he may be your little boy or mine.

Some day the world will need a man! I stand beside his cot at night
And wonder if I'm teaching him, as best I can, to know the right.
I am the father of a boy—his life is mine to make or mar—
And he no better can become than what my daily teachings are;
There will be need for someone great—I dare not falter from the line—
The man that is to serve the world may be that little boy of mine.

Perhaps your boy and mine may not ascend the lofty heights of fame;
The orders for their births are hid. We know not why to earth they came.
Yet in some little bed tonight the great man of tomorrow sleeps
And only He who sent him here, the secret of his purpose keeps.
As fathers then our care is this—to keep in mind the Great Design.
The man the world shall need some day may be your little boy or mine.

a desperate struggle, saved it from drowning and carried it, unharmed, to its mother. Do you not think that was a very noble deed?"

"My son," said the Persian, "you did only your duty. It was your duty to save the child. You, too, have acted well, but not nobly."

Then the youngest son said, "I had an enemy who has tried many times to kill me. One day, I was traveling along a very narrow and dangerous road. On one side was a high mountain, and on the other a steep, high cliff. I was surprised to see someone lying in the road. I dismounted and found that it was my enemy.

"He was asleep on the very edge of the cliff. If he had moved in his sleep, he would have rolled over and been dashed to pieces on the rocks below. I might have pushed him over, but I pulled him back, woke him, and sent him on his way."

Then the father cried out in joy. "Dear Son, the diamond is yours. For to do good to those who would do us evil is a noble and generous deed that few men are wise enough and strong enough to perform."

Famous Fathers
By Amy Puetz

Test your knowledge about famous fathers. Match the question on the left with the correct man on the right. Answers are below.

1. This man fought during the American Revolution and his son, Robert, served as a general during the Civil War.
2. This man became a father at the age of one hundred.
3. This man shot an apple off this son's head.
4. This explorer left his son Diego at the Spanish court.
5. This man never actually had children but he raised his stepchildren and great grandchildren with his wife Martha.
6. This man was the patriarch of the twelve tribes of Israel.
7. This president loved living in the White House with his four sons and two daughters.
8. This president served during the Civil War. His son Willie died in 1862. His other son Tad often brightened the gloomy days of the war for his father.

A. William Tell
B. George Washington
C. Christopher Columbus
D. Jacob
E. Abraham Lincoln
F. Henry "Light Horse Harry" Lee
G. Abraham
H. Theodore Roosevelt

Answers 1-F, 2-G, 3-A, 4-C, 5-B, 6-D, 7-H, 8-E

Independence Day
July 4

The long history leading up to the American War for Independence is too in-depth to cover in this short sketch, but the colonies of North America tried repeatedly to have a peaceful reconciliation with Britain. The events of Lexington and Concord in April of 1775 showed the Americans that Britain did not want to give them freedom. Boston was controlled by the English, and the Continental Congress met in Philadelphia to decide the fate of their land.

When everything else failed, the leaders in America gathered together and prepared a document that declared their independence from the mother country. Five men—Thomas Jefferson, John Adams, Benjamin Franklin, Roger Sherman, and Robert Livingston—were asked to write the Declaration of Independence. On July 2, 1776, the Declaration was adopted but many debates and changes took place until July 4, when it was officially adopted. On July 5, copies of the Declaration were dispatched to the states and army. It was not until August 2 that most of the leaders signed. The last person to sign was Thomas McKean in 1781. July 4, 1776 became the birthday of the United States.

Since that time, the United States has set aside this special day to remember the sacrifice of our ancestors in the cause of freedom. Many of the men who signed the Declaration really did give their lives, fortunes, and sacred honor to give us liberty.

The stories in this section show the bravery of the men and women who won the independence that was declared. Some are well-known others are not. There are also short biographical sketches of the signers. To learn more about the men who signed the Declaration of Independence *Lives of the Signers* by Benson J. Lossing is a good resource. The story on July 4 shows how people in the early 1900s celebrated the Fourth.

SIGNING OF THE DECLARATION BY JOHN TRUMBULL

June 21

A Famous Writing Desk
By Albert Blaisdell, 1913

The War of the American Revolution began in 1775. Up to that time, the colonies in this country were subject to England. In 1760 George the Third, a young man of twenty-two, came to the English throne. He needed money and listened to the advice of unwise men.

"Tax the Americans," they urged, "Make them pay on everything they receive in our ships; they are rich and will not mind it."

King George tried another way also to force money out of the colonists. A law was made that every piece of paper on which legal notes, deeds, and such things were written, should have a stamp on it. Even the almanacs and the newspapers had to have stamps on them. Some stamps cost one cent and others were fifty cents.

This law was called the Stamp Act. It made the people very angry. In Virginia, a great and bold patriot named Patrick Henry told the people to use any paper they pleased and pay no heed to the new law. The people made up their minds not to submit to such taxation. They refused to buy the stamps and burned all they could get. On the day the law went into effect, shops were closed, church bells tolled, and flags were placed at half-staff.

Not long after this, the English king issued a tax on glass, paper, tea, and other things.

The trouble between the king and his American subjects grew more and more bitter.

"Pay the taxes," King George insisted, "or I will send my soldiers and make you."

Our people replied that it was not the amount of the tax that they cared for. They claimed that King George had no right to tax them at all without their consent, and they declared over and over that they would not obey.

True to his word, King George sent soldiers to force the people to submit. Two regiments of redcoats were quartered or stationed in Boston.

This, of course, made our people very angry. They hated the soldiers and called them bad names. The soldiers paid back insult with insult.

One day, a number of angry schoolboys complained to the British commander that the redcoats had destroyed their sledding on Boston Common.

"The very children here," remarked General Gage to one of his officers, "draw in a love of liberty with the air they breathe."

Signers of the Declaration

William Floyd

1734 – 1821
Landowner
Wives* – Hannah Jones and Joanna Strong
Children – 8
State – New York

This signer from New York owned a large estate on Long Island called Mastic. His wife (Hannah) and children had to leave their home when the British moved through the area. It would be seven years before they returned. Hannah died shortly after escaping from the British. The British plundered his home and used it as a barrack when they occupied Long Island. He supported the Constitution and served as a Representative to Congress.

*AFTER HIS FIRST WIFE DIED HE REMARRIED. MANY OF THE SIGNERS WERE WIDOWERS WHO MARRIED A SECOND TIME. THIS IS THE CASE EACH TIME 'WIVES' ARE MENTIONED IN THE SIDEBARS.

Francis Lewis

1713–1802
Occupation - Merchant
Wife – Elizabeth Annesley
Children – 3
State – New York

Francis Lewis was born in Wales and came to America to set up a merchant business. He was imprisoned by the French during the French and Indian War. As a reward for his service, the British government gave him land in America. His home on Long Island was ransacked by the British. His wife, Elizabeth, was imprisoned and treated harshly. Eventually the British released her but she died a short time later. His son served during the war and later became the governor of New York.

Then a quarrel arose one evening in Boston between the soldiers and the people. The soldiers fired into the crowd, and five people were killed and seven wounded.

The bells of the city were rung, and the roar of angry voices filled the narrow streets. Quiet was not restored until the troops were sent to a fort in the harbor.

Three years later, King George took the tax off everything except tea. He said he kept this to show the Yankees he had a right to tax them.

Ship after ship filled with tea were sent to this country, but not a pound of it was allowed to be sold. Hundreds of chests were stored in damp cellars and left to spoil. Some of the ships carried their cargoes back to England.

One winter day in 1773, two ships came to Boston, but they were not allowed to unload their tea. In the night, a party of men, dressed like Indians, rushed on board the vessel, broke open the chests (three hundred and forty-two in all) and threw their contents into the sea.

Of course the king was very angry. More troops were sent, and affairs went rapidly from bad to worse.

Wise men all over the land saw that war must come. Guns and gunpowder were made ready. Hundreds of men formed themselves into companies to fight at a minute's notice.

War broke out shortly afterward. It began with the Battle of Lexington on April 19, 1775. A few weeks later, a hard-fought battle took place on Bunker Hill.

We must not forget that our people called themselves loyal British subjects during this time. They had fought as Englishmen for their rights, and not against England.

Slowly but surely, however, the idea of independence began to grow. Men saw that they were really fighting for freedom. Public meetings were called, and the question was talked over. Some of the best men in the colonies were sent to Philadelphia to attend a meeting there. On that occasion, a staunch patriot from Virginia offered a resolution, saying, "These united colonies are, and of a right ought to be, a free and independent state,"

Five of the ablest men of the country were selected to prepare a statement for publication. Thomas Jefferson of Virginia, chairman of this committee, was chosen to draw up the paper. He was not a strong public speaker, but he was known as a writer of plain and simple English.

Jefferson had rented rooms of a cabinet maker named Ben Randall, and it seems that he planned a writing desk and had Mr. Randall make it for him. It was a plain little

Signers of the Declaration

Philip Livingston

1716 – 1778
Merchant
Wife – Christina Ten Broeck
Children – 9
State – New York

Philip Livingston graduated from Yale College. This wealthy merchant from New York owned two houses that were captured by the British. One they used as a barrack, and the other as a Royal Navy hospital. After Washington's defeat on Long Island, he met his officers at this delegate's home on Brooklyn Heights to discuss plans for a retreat. Livingston tried to be a peacemaker between England and America until it became apparent that things had gone too far, then he heartily joined with the Americans. He died during the Revolution.

affair of mahogany and stood only about three inches high from the table on which it was placed.

Well, this desk has come to be famous, for on it Jefferson wrote that wonderful document known as the Declaration of Independence.

When Jefferson had finished the writing, he invited Benjamin Franklin to call at his room to hear what he had written.

"That's good enough. I wish I had written it myself. That will make King George gnash his teeth," said the genial old gentleman, when the different passages were read to him.

There was a lively debate when the Declaration was presented to the delegates at Philadelphia. With a few slight changes, however, it was finally adopted. It was signed on July 4, 1776.

We may be sure it was a time of deep interest to the hundreds gathered outside the Old State House on that hot July afternoon. The old bell ringer had been in the belfry since morning, having placed a boy in the hall below to wait for the signal.

"They will never do it, they will never do it!" cried the old bell ringer, impatiently shaking his head.

Suddenly a shout came from below. The boy, wild with excitement, came running up the belfry stairs, calling out, "Ring! Ring!"

And the old man rang the bell as it had never been rung before.

Riders on the swiftest horses carried the glad news far and wide. Cannons were fired, bells were rung, patriotic music was played, flags were flung to the breeze, and bonfires were lighted on hills and mountains.

Look at a copy of the Declaration of Independence and see the big bold signature of John Hancock of Massachusetts.

"There!" exclaimed this great patriot. "King George can read that without spectacles."

Stephen Hopkins of Rhode Island was sick at this time, his name is written with a shaky hand. "See how my hand trembles," he said, "but my heart does not."

"We must all hang together in this matter," were the words of John Hancock, when they crowded around the table to sign their names to the document.

"Surely," replied the witty Benjamin Franklin, "we must indeed, or we shall all hang separately."

All honor goes to the fifty-six bold patriots who signed the Declaration of Independence. They staked "their lives, their fortunes, and their sacred honor." They were chosen men of high purpose and exalted character. They were fit to become the leaders of the young nation.

Thomas Jefferson's Declaration of Independence is now in Washington. It has become worn and faded, but is preserved as a most sacred document.

As for the little mahogany writing desk, it too has found its way to Washington, to rest with other precious relics of colonial days. When Jefferson was an old man, he gave the desk to his granddaughter. It remained in her family until recently when it was presented to Congress and became the property of the nation.

The Tricolor Game
By Mary Dawson, 1916 and Amy Puetz

Having chosen partners, give each team one of each card below. The cards may be held together by punching a hole in one of the corners and threading a ribbon through them. On each card, allusions to the color it represents are to be written, the partners assisting each other in thinking up such allusions. A certain time should be allotted for thinking up the terms, say five to ten minutes. A timer may be set. Examples of the allusions, which may include quotations, book titles, etc. follow to illustrate the idea:

Red—*Red Badge of Courage*, red apple, redwood, Red Cross, red bird, etc.

White—The white ship, The White House, Snow White, whitewash, Whitechapel.

Blue—The blues, blue blood, blue stocking, blue beard, blueberry, bluebell.

The team who comes up with the most words wins! If they come up with more than twelve the back of the card may be used too. Instead of having just two people on a team, the teams may be made up of groups of three or four.

Red	White	Blue
1. _____	1. _____	1. _____
2. _____	2. _____	2. _____
3. _____	3. _____	3. _____
4. _____	4. _____	4. _____
5. _____	5. _____	5. _____
6. _____	6. _____	6. _____
7. _____	7. _____	7. _____
8. _____	8. _____	8. _____
9. _____	9. _____	9. _____
10. _____	10. _____	10. _____
11. _____	11. _____	11. _____
12. _____	12. _____	12. _____

June 22

The Flag of Their Regiment

By Carolyn Sherwin Bailey, 1917

rudence looked up from her sewing. It was a pleasant place to work, out there in the morning sunshine that trickled through the big white pillars of the broad piazza. The wide street was overarched by the leafy branches of the spreading elms, but the houses that lined the streets were strangely empty of life.

It was in Philadelphia in the long, long-ago time of the Revolution. Prudence was a quaint, demure little patriot girl. In all her eleven years she had known nothing save the daily routine of the simple home: the scouring of floors, the polishing of copper kettles and brass andirons and mahogany chairs, the making of huge loaves of bread and yellow butter and round cheeses, the bleaching of linen, and the patching together of bright blocks of colored cloth to make log cabin and morning star bed quilts.

Sometimes there was a quilting bee or donation party at the minister's to attend. These, with their feasts of rich preserves and pound cake, and the children's table set after the grownups had finished, were wonderful parties for Prudence. Usually, though, her days were very much alike. She helped her mother and studied her lessons from school books in wooden covers, and stitched her sampler when the studying was done. It was not a cross-stitch sampler, though, that Prudence was working on so busily now. Her needle flew in and out as she stitched together some long, straight strips of red calico and white cotton. In her lap lay some star-shaped pieces of plain white cotton calico. The edges were neatly turned in and basted, ready for sewing upon a square of blue calico cloth that Prudence had just cut.

"Put up your work! It's too pleasant a day to sew."

Prudence looked up and saw a boy standing in front of her—her neighbor, William Brewster. They had the same round, rosy faces. Prudence's short-sleeved, short-waisted frock and William's ruffled shirt were both cut from the same cloth. It was green and white gingham from Deacon Wells' store. From beneath William's long trousers and Prudence's skirt showed the same stout shoes with copper tips on the toes.

William ran up the steps of the piazza and pulled Prudence's sewing.

"Oh, William!" Prudence gasped. "Be careful! You'll soil the white cotton I fear. What ails your hands? I never saw them so stained before in all my life."

William dropped down on the top step and held up his two brown hands in the sunlight, laughing merrily.

Signers of the Declaration

Stephen Hopkins

1707–1785
Occupation – Merchant
Wives – Sarah Scott and Anna Smith
Children – 7
State – Rhode Island

Stephen Hopkins was a Quaker. He was the only one wearing a hat in Trumbull's painting. In 1774 he wanted to see slavery abolished in his native state, he even freed all his slaves. He had a unique signature that looks as if he was trembling in fear when he did it. He actually had palsy. He said, "My hand trembles, but my heart does not!" He helped create the Articles of Confederation.

John Penn

1740–1788
Occupation – Lawyer
Wife – Susannah Lyme
Children – 3
State – North Carolina

John Penn was a self-taught lawyer. He was born in Virginia and moved to North Carolina in 1774. He signed the Articles of Confederation as well as the Declaration.

Signers of the Declaration
Samuel Adams

1722–1803
Occupation – Merchant
Wives – Elizabeth Checkley
and Elizabeth Wells
Children – 6
State – Massachusetts

When Paul Revere made his midnight ride to warn the Americans about the coming of the British, he also wanted to warn Samuel Adams and John Hancock that the British planned to capture them in their hideout. Samuel Adams was called the "Father of the American Revolution." He helped form the "committees of correspondence" after the Boston Massacre to help the American people stay connected. He helped plan the Boston Tea Party. At the Old South Meeting House, he said, "This meeting can do no more to save the country." This was the signal for the men to head for the wharf to dump the tea overboard. The first Conventional Congress met in 1774. It was suggested that the convention open with prayer but some of the members were opposed to this because of their different theological views. Adams spoke up and said he was willing to hear a prayer from any gentleman who was virtuous and a friend of his country. He moved that they request a local minister to open the next day with prayer. He once said, "Neither the wisest constitution nor the wisest laws will secure the liberty and happiness of a people whose manners are universally corrupt."

"You are indeed right, Prudence," he said. "My hands need a dose of my mother's good soft soap, but," the boy's voice dropped to a whisper, "all this morning I have been busy digging holes in the orchard."

"Why?" Prudence's blue eyes were wide with wonder. William got up now and looked all about him to see that no one was listening. Then he whispered in Prudence's ear.

"For burying the silver," he explained. "We packed it all in a strong box: my grandmother's teaspoons, the silver cake basket with the design of strawberries around the edge, and the sugar tongs. We buried them all oh very deeply."

"Was it necessary, William?" Prudence's eyes were frightened as she spoke. "I know that my mother, before she had to take to her bed with the ague (a cold accompanied by shivering and fever), planned to hide our silver in the well that is dried out. Are—are, the redcoats, coming through Philadelphia soon?"

"They do say that they are coming. I am very fearful," William answered. Then, as Prudence's pink cheeks grew a little pale at the thought, the boy pointed to her sewing.

"What are you stitching, Prudence? Surely you are not going to dress yourself in these gaudy colors? It would scarcely be right in these hard times."

Prudence laughed, shaking out the strips of scarlet and white that filled her lap.

"No, indeed, William. Dark colors and plain frocks must be worn by us children of the war. I am making a flag. Our great, beautiful stars and stripes of the United States went to our regiment with Father and your brother John. But I went down to the flag shop of Mrs. Betsy Ross not long ago, and I stood awhile on the threshold, watching how she and her maids cut and sewed their red, white, and blue cloth together. I said to myself, "Why not make your own flag, Prudence Williams? You have ten fingers and a piece bag up in the attic. And here it is, all done but sewing on the little white stars."

"Oh, Prudence!" William's eyes shone.

"It is wonderful! How did you ever measure and sew it so well? I always did say that you are the most clever girl with your needle of any in town."

"It is carefully made," Prudence assented, "but that is because I thought of my regiment with every stitch. And I wished that I might march in the regiment beside my father, waving my flag, and shouting for the independence of our dear country at every step."

"It would be grand," William said, "but now let's go in the house and delve in your cookie crock, Prudence.

Perhaps your cook has filled it with her good caraway cakes," and the two little neighbors disappeared through the great white door of the old house.

In the days that followed, Prudence quite forgot to dread the coming to Philadelphia of the British soldiers. Rumors came of how the redcoats had marched through the nearby towns and countryside. They had taken possession of the homesteads, appropriated the supplies that had been left for the women and children, and plundered the treasures of silver that were almost all the wealth of the people. News of this reached the ears of those who remained behind, alone, in Philadelphia. But Prudence paid little heed to the rumors. Her mother was better, but still an invalid and confined to her room. There was only one maidservant to do the work of the large house, and Prudence found herself a real little housekeeper with her hands very full. All day long she tripped up and down the wide oak staircase, with instructions from her dear mother to the maid in the kitchen, and then helped to carry them out. She had finished the flag. It was laid away in a drawer.

"It's hardly safe to fly a flag from your piazza, Prudence," sensible William had warned. So Prudence opened the drawer only when she had a little spare time. Then she would kneel down on the rag carpet in front of the drawer and hold the beloved Stars and Stripes tenderly in her arms.

"I love every star, and every color," she would say to herself. "Oh, may God win the battle for us and help to give me back my father, and William his brother John!"

The next morning, when Prudence set the tray with her mother's breakfast, she laid it with unusual care. Upon the sun-bleached linen cloth stood the thin china dishes, white with a pattern of raised bunches of grapes in purple and green. The silver spoons and forks were arranged neatly. Prudence's mother, sitting in a big armchair by the window where the sweet odors of the garden roses were blown up to her, looked lovingly at her small daughter.

"You are a good little housekeeper my dear," she said. "I don't know what I should have done without you. Father will find his little girl almost a little woman when he returns." She paused a moment, lifting one of the silver spoons to break the end of her eggshell. "If he ever does return," she sighed. "Oh, I should have hidden the silver weeks ago." The sound of a muffled drum struck her ear. She looked at Prudence in terror. "Pull the curtains closed, child, and lock all the doors. The redcoats are coming."

Like a line of fire taking its winding way in and out between the houses, the regiment of British soldiers

Samuel Huntington

1731–1796
Occupation – Lawyer
Wife – Martha Devotion
Children – 2 adopted
State – Connecticut

Samuel Huntington learned the trade of a cooper but taught himself to become a lawyer. He signed the Articles of Confederation. He served as the first president of congress when the Articles of Confederation were signed. Some people think of him as the first president of the United States instead of Washington. He served as the governor of Connecticut from 1786–96 and issued a proclamation for a day of thanksgiving in 1788. It said, "To offer up fervent supplication and prayer to Almighty God, the Supreme Governor of the Universe, and ruler of the Kingdoms of Men, that it may graciously please Him to shower divine blessings upon the people of these United States."

streamed through the streets of Philadelphia. Here it stopped as an officer, and his men stripped the fruit from some peaceful orchard or garden. There, at an officer's order, a group of soldiers entered a house and returned with bits of old family treasure that war gave them the privilege of taking.

Prudence's heart beat fast, but she tried to be brave. She ran from room to room, stowing away the silver candlesticks and tableware, closing blinds, and locking doors. The old maidservant, her apron held over her head, had fled to the cellar in her fright. Her mother, bravely directing Prudence, was still unable to leave her room. Suddenly the front door burst open and in came William.

"I couldn't bear to leave you alone, Prudence," he said. "See, I brought my father's old drum, thinking we could make a little noise on it and scare the redcoats."

Prudence looked into the brave face of her little neighbor.

"You've given me an idea, William," she exclaimed. She ran over to the chest of drawers, opened one drawer, and pulled out the little homemade flag.

"We'll both scare the redcoats," she said. "We won't fasten the doors, for it wouldn't be of any use. The soldiers could very easily break the bolts, and I can't find any safe place to hide the silver. Come, we'll go right out on the piazza and meet the whole British army if it comes!" She clutched William's hand and tugged him toward the door.

"Do we dare?" William's round, merry face was very sober.

"Of course we dare. Come on. You drum, and I'll wave the Stars and Stripes," Prudence said.

The Williams' white house, set a little back from the street in the midst of sweet old flower beds and low hedges of box and yew, looked like a prize to the ruthless redcoats. It was well known in Philadelphia at that time that Prudence's father had used much of his wealth to further the cause of independence. This made the invading enemy hate him. It was a common rumor, too, that although the Williams' chests of gold were greatly depleted, there was still much treasure of silver left in the home. News of it passed from mouth to mouth of the soldiers.

"There's the house. Left flank, wheel, halt!" shouted the British general in command. He turned in at the Williams' gate and strode up the path. At the steps, he looked up and stopped. "Goodness!" he said. "The children of these stubborn colonists would defy us, too." But a smile took away the stern lines from his mouth.

On the top step of the piazza stood Prudence and William, two brave little patriots. William was beating a loud *rap tap* on the cracked head of an old drum. Prudence, her arm held high above her head, waved the little homemade flag that showed the glorious Stars and Stripes of their regiment.

"You mustn't come a step farther, Sir!" she commanded.

"No indeed!" echoed William. "We won't let you come in."

"So you're holding the fort, are you?" the general asked.

"We have to, Sir," Prudence explained. "My father is with the Continental army and my mother is ill. This is my neighbor, William Brewster. He came over to help me guard the house." Then she turned pleading eyes toward the great man as she held out her flag.

"It looks to me as if there were a thousand redcoats, Sir, more or less, out there in the road. There are only two of us. Please, Sir, for the sake of our flag, march on!"

Was it dust or the mist of tears that made the British general wipe his eyes? He reached out one ungloved hand and grasped Prudence's little one.

"Give my sympathy to your mother, my child," he said kindly, "and tell her that I hope she will soon be better. Little soldiers, remember that never before have I surrendered, but now I do so in the name of the king. March on!" he ordered to his men. Looking back he saw Prudence and William standing in the gate and waving him goodbye until the trees, and the distance shut them from his view.

Yankee Doodle

This was one of the most popular songs of the American Revolution. Sing it today.

1. Fath'r and I went down to camp A-
2. And there was Cap-tain Wash-ing-ton Up-
3. And there they had a swamp-ing gun, As
4. And ev-'ry time they fired it off it
5. And there they'd fife a-way like fun, And
6. But I can't tell you half I see, They

long with Cap-tain Good-win, And there we saw the
on a slap-ping stal-lion A giv-ing or-ders
big as a log of ma-ple On a deu-ced
took a horn of pow-der; It made a noise like
play on corn-stalk fid-dles, And some had rib-bons
kept up such a smo-ther; So I took off,

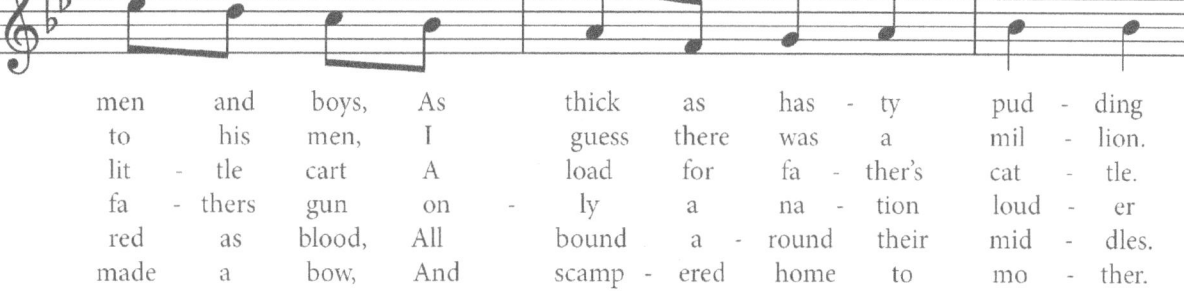

men and boys, As thick as has-ty pud-ding
to his men, I guess there was a mil-lion.
lit-tle cart A load for fa-ther's cat-tle.
fa-thers gun on-ly a na-tion loud-er
red as blood, All bound a-round their mid-dles.
made a bow, And scamp-ered home to mo-ther.

Chorus:
Yan-kee doo-dle keep it up, Yan-kee doo-dle dan-dy,

Mind the mu-sic and the step, and with the girls be hand-y

Summer Countdown   **Amy Puetz**

June 23

The General's Daughter
By James Johonnot, 1914

Tempe Hides Her Horse
By Mr. Blaisdell and Mr. Ball, 1911

The General's Daughter
By James Johonnot, 1914

In the year 1781, the war was chiefly carried on in the South, but the North was constantly troubled by bands of Tories and Indians, who would swoop down on small settlements and make off with whatever they could lay their hands on.

During this time, General Schuyler was staying at his house, which stood just outside the stockade or walls of Albany. The British commander sent out a party of Tories and Indians to capture the general.

When they reached the outskirts of the city, they learned from a Dutch laborer that the general's house was guarded by six soldiers, three watching by night and three by day. They let the Dutchman go, and as soon as the band was out of sight he hastened to Albany and warned the general of their approach.

Schuyler gathered his family in one of the upper rooms of his house, and giving orders that the doors and windows should be barred, fired a pistol from a top story window to alarm the neighborhood.

The soldiers on guard, who had been lounging under a tree, started to their feet at the sound of the pistol, but, alas, too late, for they found themselves surrounded by a crowd of dusky forms, who bound them hand and foot before they had time to resist.

In the room upstairs was the sturdy general, standing resolutely at the door, with gun in hand, while his slaves were gathered about him, each with a weapon. At the other end of the room, the women were huddled together, some weeping and some praying.

Suddenly, a deafening crash was heard. The Indian band had broken into the house. With loud shouts, they began to pillage and to destroy everything in sight. While they were yet busy downstairs, Mrs. Schuyler sprang to her feet and rushed to the door, for she had suddenly remembered that the baby, who was only a few months old, was asleep in its cradle in a room on the first floor.

The general caught his wife in his arms and implored her not to go to certain death, saying that if anyone were to go he would. While this generous struggle between husband and wife was going on, their daughter, Margarita, who had been standing near the door, glided by them and descended the stairs.

All was dark in the hall, except where the light shone from the dining room in which the Indians were pillaging the shelves and fighting over their booty. How to get passed the dining room door was the question, but the brave young lady did not hesitate. Reaching the lower hall, she walked very deliberately forward, softly but quickly passing the door and, unobserved, reached the room with the cradle.

She caught up her baby sister, crept back past the open door, and was just mounting the stairs when one of the Indians happened to see her. "Whiz" and his sharp tomahawk struck the stair rail within a few inches of the baby's head and tore Margarita's dress. But the frightened young lady hurried on and in a few seconds, was safe in her father's arms.

As for the Indians, fearing an attack from the nearby garrison, they hastened away with the booty they had collected and left General Schuyler and his family unharmed.

Margarita's older sister Elizabeth married Alexander Hamilton.

Tempe Hides Her Horse
By Mr. Blaisdell and Mr. Ball, 1911

The War of the Revolution had been going on for two years. Washington and his army were in camp near Morristown, New Jersey, not far from New York City. The British army was in camp nearby.

A little distance away was an estate known as the Wicks' farm. On it lived its owner, Mr. Wicks, with an invalid wife and an only daughter, a young girl named Temperance. She was called Tempe for short. She owned a fine horse named Flora.

Now that there was war in the land, stragglers from both armies were making no end of trouble. Still, the young girl rode here and there and everywhere without fear, just as she had done in times of peace.

"Washington's soldiers will do me no harm," thought Tempe, "and I am sure my Flora can run faster than any horse the redcoats have. Let them catch me if they can."

It was a lovely afternoon in June, and Tempe was returning home through the woods after a long ride. She was within a mile or so of the farm. All of a sudden, from a clump of bushes beside the road, stepped out a dozen British soldiers.

"Halt, young woman!" cried the sergeant.

She looked round in surprise. There were the redcoats drawn up in line, aiming their guns at her. The girl spoke to her horse, and the faithful animal stopped. Up rushed the soldiers and seized the bridle.

"What do you want of me?" asked Tempe. "This horse is mine, and I am on my way home. You have no right to stop me."

"Never mind, miss, this is a fine horse of yours," and the sergeant took a good look at Flora.

"She certainly is, but she belongs to me, and I must ride home at once. So let me go."

"Not so fast, young lady," continued the officer. "This is just the horse my captain wants; his own horse died last week."

"I don't care anything about your captain and what he wants," cried Tempe, getting a little angry. "Go about your business and let me get home."

"I have orders to take horses wherever I find them," was the calm reply of the officer, "so, young miss, jump down!"

Signers of the Declaration
Lewis Morris

1726–1798
Occupation – Planter
Wife – Mary Walton
Children – 10
State – New York

Lewis Morris owned a large estate called Morrisania, which the British pillaged. His family had to flee from their estate when the British marched through. He served as a major-general in the New York militia. He had three sons who fought under Washington in the American Revolution. He helped promote the ratification of the Constitution in his state.

The girl saw that the redcoats were in earnest and were bound to rob her of her horse. She was keen-witted and quickly made up her mind what to do. She pretended to be getting ready to dismount. The redcoat who held the bridle let go of it, and turned aside for a moment to speak to a comrade. Quick as a flash the girl gave the spirited horse a cut with her whip, dashed between two of the soldiers, and was gone.

"Fire, men, fire!" shouted the sergeant.

Bang! Bang! Bang!

The soldiers had fired their guns into the air, thinking to make the girl stop.

It was too late. Tempe was far down the road, riding as fast as the swift horse could carry her. The redcoats did not give up the chase. Some of them knew where the girl lived. They ran through the woods, hoping to reach the Wicks' farm first.

"What shall I do with Flora when I get her home?" Tempe wrinkled her pretty brow. "There are no men to help me, and these redcoats will be sure to go to the barn and carry her off. What shall I do?"

She could ride over to one of the neighbors, but sooner or later she would have to come back. The redcoats would watch for her, even if it took a week. If she tied her horse to a tree in the woods and came back on foot, the soldiers would soon find the animal's hiding place.

Tempe did some lively thinking while she was riding home. An idea came to her just as she was within sight of the house. She looked down the road. The redcoats were not in sight.

Not a moment was to be lost. She dashed through the front gate of the large yard and jumped from her horse at the back door. Opening the door, she led the gentle animal through the kitchen into the front hall, and then into the parlor.

Now off the parlor was a bedroom, which was a guest chamber. There was only one window, and the shutters were closed when the room was not in use. Into this dark room, Tempe quickly led her horse and tied her to the bedpost.

Hardly had the young girl made everything snug when the angry soldiers came tramping into the yard. They searched the big barn, the carriage house, and the woodshed. At last, they came into the kitchen.

"Where did you hide that horse, young girl?" growled the sergeant. "Tell us, or there will be trouble."

"Very well!" smiled Tempe. "But if you get my horse, you will have to find her first."

Signers of the Declaration

William Ellery

1727–1820
Occupation – Lawyer and Merchant
Wives – Ann Remington
and Abigail Carey
Children – 16
State – Rhode Island

His home was destroyed by the British. He tried to have slavery abolished in 1785.

Button Gwinnett

1735–1777
Occupation – Merchant and Planter
Wife – Anne Bourne
Children – 3
State – Georgia

Button Gwinnett's odd first name was actually his mother's maiden name. He owned a home on St. Catherine's Island off the coast of Georgia. During the war, he and his family would often have to flee to the mainland because the English would stop at the island to take loose livestock. He died after fighting a duel in 1777.

Angry words were of no use, and at last the redcoats gave up the search and rode back to their camp. They never imagined that the horse was hidden in the house and quietly eating her oats in the best bedroom. The noise of her feet had been muffled with a feather bed.

As the story goes, Tempe kept her horse in the bedroom for three weeks. Shortly afterward, the British troops broke up their camp in New Jersey and went back to New York. Not one of them, however, rode on Tempe's horse. When the redcoats had gone, Flora came out of the guest chamber and went back to her stall in the big barn.

Our Own Dear Land by J. R. Thomas, 1920

Our own dear land, our native land,
Home of the brave and free!
In vain we search old ocean's strand
To find a land like thee.
Thy towering hills, thy prairies wide,
Thy forests old and dim,
Thy streams that roll in matchless prides
Thy torrent's thunder-hymn.

Our own dear land, our native land,
None can compare with thee;
The fairest work of nature's hand.
Our own dear land for me!

Our own dear land, our native land,
Fearless thy banner waves,
And nations yet unborn shall stand
Beside thy heroes' graves.

Our fathers spurned oppression's laws,
All fought for God and right;
So may their sons, in freedom's cause,
Be foremost in the fight!

Our own dear land, our native land,
Home of the brave and free;
The finest work of nature's hand.
Our own dear land for me!

Star Craft

It is easy to make 3-D stars. They are great decorations for the Fourth of July.

Make a copy of the next page and print it on red, white, and blue card stock. Cut out the star shapes and the dotted line. Slip the dotted line cuts into each other to give the star a 3-D effect. The stars may be glued to help them stay together.

You might also experiment with making some larger and some smaller. To do this, just enlarge or shrink the stars on the next page on a copy machine.

Summer Countdown   **Amy Puetz**

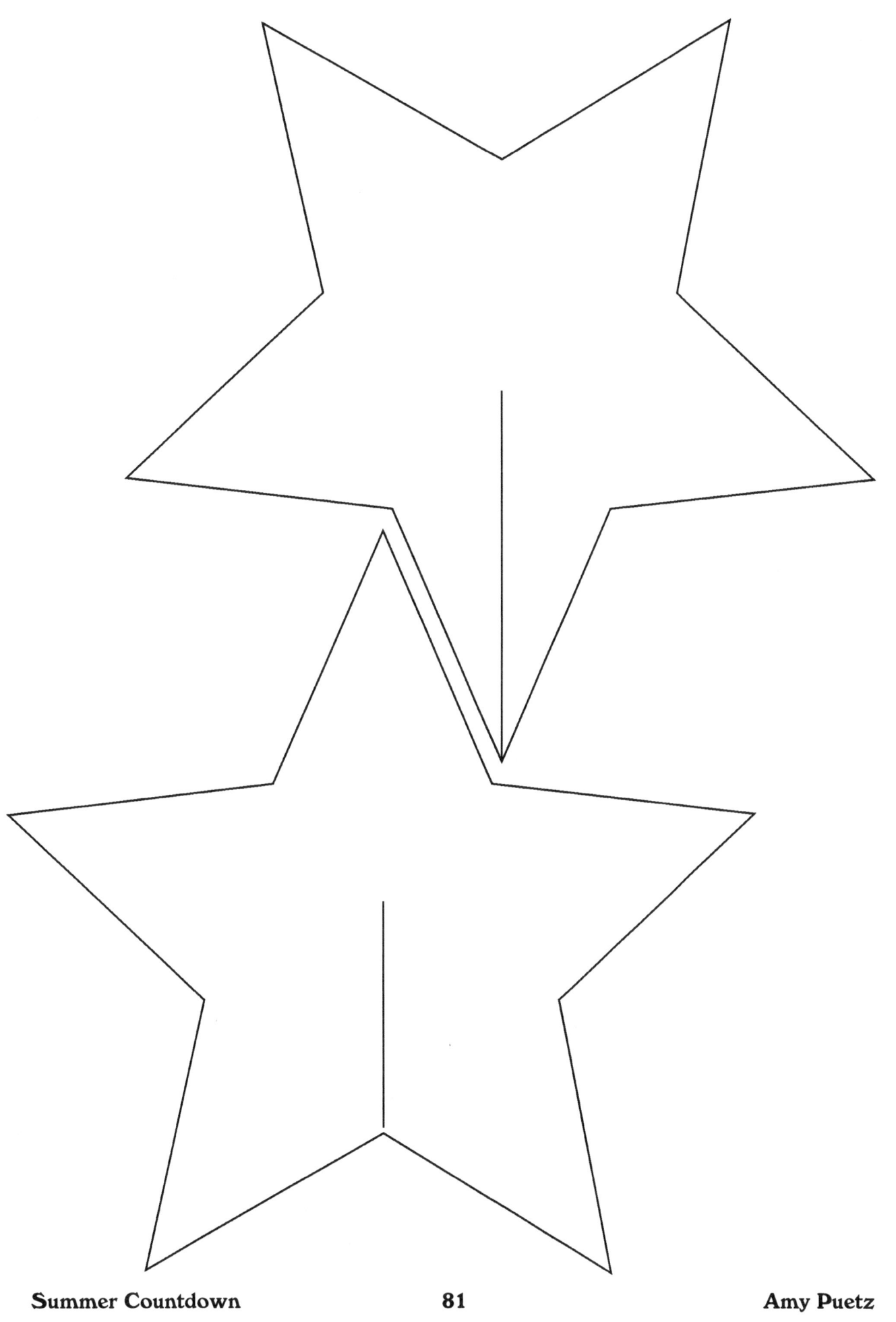

June 24

The Midnight Ride of Paul Revere

By Henry Wadsworth Longfellow, 1861
and Albert Blaisdell, 1913

In 1860, Henry Wadsworth Longfellow wrote a poem called "The Midnight Ride of Paul Revere." The story below combines the poem with the real story. ~ Amy Puetz

> Listen, my children, and you shall hear
> Of the midnight ride of Paul Revere,
> On the eighteenth of April, in seventy-five;
> Hardly a man is now alive,
> Who remembers that famous day and year.

General Gage was in command of the British forces in America. There were now about four thousand redcoats in Boston. It was plain enough that this meant war.

"If we must fight, we will get ready," said the patriots, and they created militia groups. They were ready to march at a minute's notice, and came to be called minutemen.

General Gage sent his spies far and wide to find where the gunpowder and supplies of the patriots were kept. On one trip, the redcoats looted Salem. On another raid, they seized the gunpowder in the old powder house on Winter Hill in Somerville.

About this time, the patriots began to store gunpowder, bullets, and pickaxes, besides a large amount of food and other supplies, in the village of Concord, twenty miles from Boston.

Secret societies were formed in Boston to watch the movements of the enemy. Picked men walked the streets night and day to learn of any sudden or unusual doings of the soldiers. Meetings were held to which nobody was admitted without having taken an oath on the Bible not to reveal anything that was said or done.

One of the leaders of the patriots in and about Boston was the famous Dr. Joseph Warren, who was killed at Bunker Hill. He chose Paul Revere as his right-hand man. Revere was at this time about forty years old. He was the leader of a band of thirty patriots who watched every move of the British.

General Gage now laid his plans to send soldiers by night to Concord. He wished to destroy the military supplies and capture Samuel Adams and John Hancock, who were known to be in that neighborhood. A British officer told this to a gunsmith named Jasper, who quickly sent word to Dr. Warren. A hostler named Ballard overheard a redcoat officer say, "There will be the mischief to pay tomorrow." The news was at once sent to Paul Revere. This was on the evening of the eighteenth of April.

Signers of the Declaration

Joseph Hewes

1730–1779
Occupation – Merchant
Wife – none
Children – none
State – North Carolina

Joseph Hewes never married. A few days before his wedding, the woman he planned to marry died. He thought it was too early to separate from Great Britain, but when the time came, he voted yes. He was friends with John Paul Jones and tried to get him a prominent rank in the navy. When Hewes died in 1779 all of his colleagues in congress mourned for a month.

Caesar Rodney

1728–1784
Occupation – Landowner
Wife – none
Children – none
State – Delaware

Caesar Rodney rode eighty miles to make sure Delaware voted yes. He had a cancerous growth on his nose and eventually died from cancer in 1784. Caesar Rodney was featured on the state quarter for Delaware.

Signers of the Declaration

Roger Sherman

1721–1793
Occupation – Lawyer
Wives – Elizabeth Hartwell and Rebecca Prescott
Children – 15
State – Connecticut

He signed the Articles of Association, Articles of Confederation, and the Constitution. During the Revolution, his three military age sons served with distinction. He would buy a Bible when he arrived at congress and read it while he was away from home, then he would give it to one of his children when he returned home. He was on the committee that drafted the Declaration of Independence. He served at the Constitutional Convention of 1787. His plan, called the Connecticut Compromise, helped the states work out their differences about how large and small states would be represented. His compromise suggested two houses, one that was based on population, and one that allowed two representatives from each state regardless of size. He helped make sure the new Constitution had a Bill of Rights. He said, "It is the duty of all to acknowledge that the Divine Law which requires us to love God with all our heart and our neighbor as ourselves, on pain of eternal damnation, is holy, just, and good."

The patriots now believed that the long-expected war was going to begin. The Sons of Liberty quickly carried the news to Dr. Warren. He sent for William Dawes and Paul Revere, and planned for them to ride to Lexington to spread the alarm. Paul Revere called on his friend, Captain Pulling, to arrange for a signal from the tower of the Old North Church, that he might know what direction the British troops were taking.

> He said to his friend, "If the British march
> By land or sea from the town tonight,
> Hang a lantern aloft in the belfry arch
> Of the North Church tower, as a signal light,
> One, if by land, and two, if by sea;
> And I on the opposite shore will be.
> Ready to ride and spread the alarm
> Through every Middlesex village and farm,
> For the country folk to be up and to arm."

Then he said good night and hurried to his boat, which lay near the present Craigie Bridge.

Two of his friends went to the boat with him. Out in the Charles River, the British man-of-war *Somerset* lay at anchor. Revere was afraid that the noise of the rowing might alarm the sentries, and sent one of his companions to the house of a friend for something to muffle the oars. The man quickly came back with a petticoat, which a Daughter of Liberty gave him. Revere and his friends pushed off from the Boston shore only five minutes before General Gage's order went out to allow nobody to leave the town that night.

> Then he said good night, and with muffled oar
> Silently rowed to the Charlestown shore,
> Just as the moon rose over the bay,
> Where swinging wide at her moorings lay
> The *Somerset*, British man-of-war;
> A phantom ship, with each mast and spar
> Across the moon, like a prison bar,
> And a huge black hulk, that was magnified
> By its own reflection in the tide.

Late in the night, under cover of the darkness, eight hundred British regulars went quietly to their boats and were rowed across the Charles River, which in those days widened into a bay, extending to the foot of the Common. They had acted with great secrecy, but they did not escape the vigilance of the patriots. Captain Pulling at once made for the Old North Church.

> The clocks were striking eleven.
> Meanwhile, impatient to mount and ride,
> Booted and spurred, with heavy stride
> On the opposite shore walked Paul Revere.
> Now he patted his horse's side,
> Now gazed at the landscape far and near,
> Then, impetuous, stamped the earth,
> And turned and tightened his saddle girth;
> But mostly he watched with eager search.
> The belfry tower of the Old North Church,
> As it rose above the graves on the hill.
> Lonely and spectral and somber and still.
> And lo! As he looks, on the belfry's height
> A glimmer, and then a gleam of light!
> He springs to the saddle, the bridle he turns,
> But lingers and gazes, till full on his sight
> A second lamp in the belfry burns.

Springing into the saddle, he dashed off toward Medford.

"Halt!" shouted a sharp voice. Two British troopers were standing guard under a tree in a narrow part of the road.

Revere wheeled his horse in the nick of time and made his escape into a road which ran over Winter Hill.

"The regulars are coming. The regulars are coming," he shouted as he galloped down the long hill into Medford. He stopped long enough to wake up Captain Hall, commander of the minutemen.

"Up and arm! The regulars are coming," and the rider galloped swift as the wind along the road to Arlington Centre. At the old Cooper tavern, he turned off toward Lexington.

"The regulars are coming. Up and arm!"

Men, women, and children awoke out of their sleep and rushed to the doors only to catch a glimpse of a horse and rider as they vanished out of sight along the dark road.

> A hurry of hoofs in a village street,
> A shape in the moonlight, a bulk in the dark.
> And beneath, from the pebbles, in passing, a spark
> Struck out by a steed flying fearless and fleet;
> That was all. And yet, through the gloom and the light,
> The fate of a nation was riding that night;

Signers of the Declaration

Oliver Wolcott

1726–1797
Occupation – Lawyer
Wife – Laura Collins
Children – 5
State – Connecticut

Oliver Wolcott was trained to be a doctor but became a lawyer instead. He fought in King George's War of the 1740s. He served as a general during the American Revolution and helped defeat General John Burgoyne at Saratoga in 1777. He served as the governor of his state from 1796 until his death in 1797. He once said, "Through various scenes of life, God has sustained me. May He ever be my unfailing friend; may His love cherish my soul; may my heart with gratitude acknowledge His goodness; and may my desires be to Him and to the remembrance of His name." He once said, "It is most evident that this land is under the protection of the Almighty, and that we shall be saved not by our wisdom nor by our might, but by the Lord of Hosts who is wonderful in counsel and Almighty in all His operations."

William Williams

1731–1811
Occupation – Merchant
Wife – Mary Trumbull
Children – 3
State – Connecticut

William Williams was the son of a Congregational minister and was trained for the ministry, but he became a merchant. This delegate from Connecticut knew he would be hung if the British won the war. He once told a man, "Well, if they succeed, it is pretty evident what will be my fate. I have done much to prosecute the contest, and one thing I have done, which the British will never pardon—have signed the Declaration of Independence. I shall be hung." When the man responded that he was glad he had not done anything that would anger the British if they were victorious, this signer responded, "Then, sir, you deserve to be hanged, for not having done your duty." He married Mary Trumbull, the daughter of Jonathan Trumbull, the governor of Connecticut.

And the spark struck out by that steed in his flight
Kindled the land into flame with its heat.

Shortly after midnight Revere reached Lexington and dashed to the house of the Reverend Jonas Clark, where Samuel Adams and John Hancock were sleeping. Eight men, under the command of Sergeant Munroe, were on guard.

"Don't make so much noise," said Munroe, "everybody is sound asleep."

"Noise?" shouted Revere, "You'll have noise enough before long. The British regulars are coming. I must see Mr. Hancock."

An upper window was raised.

"Never mind, Revere, come in. We aren't afraid of you," said the great man, who was now wide awake.

Half an hour later Dawes arrived from his longer ride through Roxbury and other towns. The two tired riders were given something to eat, after which they started toward Concord to spread the alarm. About two miles beyond Lexington they were captured by British officers who were on guard in the woods. Both managed to escape. Revere reached Lexington on foot about the time the first volley was fired at daybreak on Lexington Common.

The news from Boston spread like wildfire. Guns were fired and church bells rang out the alarm. Men and boys loaded their guns, put on their powder horns, filled their pockets with bullets, and marched hurriedly along the country roads toward Lexington.

Before nine o'clock hundreds of minutemen, even as far away as forty miles out of Boston, were on their way to cut off the British regulars that dreadful nineteenth of April 1775.

You know the rest. In the books you have read
How the British regulars fired and fled,
How the farmers gave them ball for ball,
From behind each fence and farmyard wall,
Chasing the redcoats down the lane,
Then crossing the fields to emerge again
Under the trees at the turn of the road,
And only pausing to fire and load.

★★★★★★★★★★★★★★★★
"No King but King Jesus."
Motto of the American Revolution
★★★★★★★★★★★★★★★★

Fruity Flag

By placing apples, blueberries, and strawberries in a rectangular dish it can give the illusion of a flag.

In the top left corner add a square or rectangular bowl with blueberries. Cut the strawberries and place them on the bottom to make the first stripe. Peel and cut the apples into eight slices. Sprinkle with lemon juice to keep the apples from turning brown. Put a row of them for the second stripe. Continue adding red and white rows.

The flag could be made up of one layer or multiple layers of fruit. Whole strawberries or sliced ones may be used.

Another idea would be to use cherry tomatoes and cut cauliflower instead of fruit for the red and white stripes. For the blue field, blueberries may still be used.

Religion and morality are the essential pillars of civil society. ~George Washington

Is life so dear, or peace so sweet, as to be purchased at the price of chains and slavery? Forbid it, Almighty God! I know not what course others may take; but as for me, give me liberty or give me death! ~Patrick Henry

If men are so wicked with religion, what would they be if without it. ~Benjamin Franklin

June 25

The Quaker Patriot
By Charles Morris, 1895

Burning Her House
By Celina Eliza Means, 1903

The Quaker Patriot
By Charles Morris, 1895

In Philadelphia, on Second Street below Spruce, formerly stood an old mansion, known by the name of Loxley's House, it having been originally the residence of Lieutenant Loxley, who served in the artillery under Braddock and took part in his celebrated defeat. During the Revolution, this house was the scene of an interesting historical incident, which is well worth relating.

At that time, it was occupied by a Quaker named Darrah, or perhaps we should say by his wife Lydia, who seems to have been the ruling spirit of the house. During the British occupation of Philadelphia, when patriots and royalists alike had to open their mansions to their enemies, the Darrah mansion was used as the quarters of the British adjutant-general. In that day, it was somewhat out of town and was frequently the scene of private conferences of the higher officers because of its seclusion.

On one chilly and snowy day, the second of December 1777, the adjutant-general appeared at the house and bade Mrs. Darrah to prepare the upper back room for a meeting of his friends, which would take place that night.

"They may stay late," he said and added emphatically, "be sure, Lydia, that your family are all in bed at an early hour. When our guests are ready to leave the house, I will give you notice, that you may let us out and extinguish the fire and candles."

Mrs. Darrah obeyed. Yet she was so struck by the mystery with which he seemed inclined to surround the projected meeting, that she made up her mind to learn, if possible, what very secret business was afoot. She obeyed his orders literally and saw that her household went to bed early, and, after receiving the officers, retired herself to her room but not to sleep. This conference might prove some peril to the American cause. If so, she wished to know it.

When she deemed the proper time had come, she removed her shoes and in stocking feet, stole softly along the passage to the door of the apartment where the officers were in consultation. Here, the keyhole served the purpose to which that useful opening has so often been put and enabled her to hear their plans. For some time, only a

Signers of the Declaration
George Read

1733–1798
Occupation – Lawyer
Wife – Gertrude Ross
Children – 5
State – Delaware

He signed the Articles of Confederation, the Declaration, and the Constitution. He voted no on the Declaration. But he still signed it once it passed and worked tirelessly for his country. He married a sister of fellow signer George Ross, named Gertrude Ross. He and his family were nearly captured by the British during the war. He was away from his family for long periods of time. His wife and children often had to flee from their house when the British were in the neighborhood. He attended the Constitutional Convention and worked in Delaware to get it ratified. Delaware was the first state to ratify the Constitution.

Signers of the Declaration

Carter Braxton
1736–1797
Occupation – Planter
Wives – Judith Robinson
and Elizabeth Corbin
Children – 18
State – Virginia

Carter Braxton opposed breaking away from England but when the time came he voted yes for independence. Before the Revolution, he served in the House of Burgesses. He owned an estate called Chericoke. His property and ships were plundered by the British. He acted as a peacemaker between the patriots and the British when the British confiscated some ammunition. A group of patriots, with Patrick Henry at their head, demanded payment or the return of their ammunition. Carter Braxton met with his father-in-law, Richard Corbin (a crown official), and settled the matter without bloodshed. The patriots were paid for the ammunition. Carter Braxton had more children than any other signer. He had 18 children, his second wife had 16 children.

John Hart
1711–1779
Occupation – Farmer
Wife – Deborah Scudder
Children – 13
State – New Jersey

John Hart's home and mill were destroyed by the Hessians. He was hunted like an outlaw by the British. He wife was ill when the Hessians attacked their farm. She died soon after. He did not live to see the victory over England. He once said, "We will look for the permanency and stability of our new government to Him who bringeth princes to nothing and teacheth senators wisdom."

murmur of voices reached her ears. Then silence fell, followed by one of the officers reading in a clear tone. She listened intently, for the document was of great interest. It was an order from Sir William Howe, arranging for a secret attack on Washington's camp at Whitemarsh. The troops were to leave the city on the night of the fourth under cover of the darkness and surprise the rebels before daybreak.

The fair eavesdropper had heard enough. Rarely had a keyhole listener been so well rewarded. She glided back to her room and threw herself on her bed. She was none too soon. In a few minutes, steps were heard in the passage and then came a rap upon her door. She was clever enough to pretend not to hear. The rap was repeated a second and a third time. Then the wise woman pretended to awake, answered in a sleepy tone, and, learning that the adjutant-general and his friends were ready to leave, arose and saw them out.

Lydia Darrah slept no more that night. The secret she had learned prevented slumber. What was to be done? This thought filled her mind the night long. Washington must be warned! But how? Should she trust her husband or some other member of her family? No, she could not put them in danger. She would trust herself alone. Before morning she had devised a plan of action and, for the first time since learning that eventful news, the anxious woman gave her mind a moment's rest.

At early dawn, she was astir. Flour was needed for the household. She woke her husband and told him of this, saying that she must make an early journey to Frankford to supply the needed stores. This was a matter of ordinary occurrence in those days, the people of Philadelphia being largely dependent upon the Frankford mills for their flour and being obliged to go for it themselves. Mr. Darrah advised that she should take the maid with her, but she declined. "The maid could not be spared from her household duties," she said.

It was a cold December morning. The snow of the day before had left several inches of its white blanket upon the ground. It was no very pleasant journey which lay before Mrs. Darrah. Frankford was some five miles away, and she was obliged to travel this distance on foot and return over the same route with her load of flour. Certainly comfort was not the ruling consideration in those days of our forefathers. A ten-mile walk through the snow for a bag of flour was not for the faint hearted.

On foot, and bag in hand, Mrs. Darrah started on her journey through the almost untrodden snow, stopping at General Howe's headquarters, on Market Street near Sixth, to obtain the requisite passport to leave the city. It was still early in the day when the devoted woman reached the mills. The British outposts did not extend to this point; those of the Americans were not far beyond. Leaving her bag at the mill to be filled, Mrs. Darrah pushed on through the wintry air, ready to incur any danger or discomfort if, thereby, she could tell the patriot army the important information which she had learned.

Fortunately, she had not far to go. After walking a short distance, she met Lieutenant-Colonel Craig, who had been sent out by Washington on a scouting expedition in search of information. She told him her story, begged him to hasten to Washington with the momentous tidings and not to reveal her name, and hurried back to the mill. Here, she shouldered the bag of flour and trudged her five miles home, arriving in as reasonably short a time as could have been expected.

Night came. The next day passed. They were a night and day of anxious suspense for Lydia Darrah. From her window, when night had again fallen, she watched anxiously for movements of the British troops. Ah, there at length they go, long lines of them, marching steadily through the darkness, but as noiselessly as possible, so as not to arouse any patriot spies.

When morning dawned, the restless woman was on the watch again. The roll of a drum came to her ears from a distance. Soon afterward troops appeared, weary and discontented warriors marching back. They had made their night's journey in vain. Instead of finding the Americans off their guard and an easy prey, they had found them wide awake, and ready to give them the hottest kind of a reception. After maneuvering about their lines for a vulnerable point and finding none, the hardy British warriors turned on their track and marched homeward.

The army authorities were all confused. How had their plans become known? Had it come from the Darrah house? Possibly, for there the conference had been held. The adjutant-general hastened to his quarters, summoned Lydia to his room, and turned to her with a stern and doubting face.

"Were any of your family up, Lydia," he asked, "on the night when I had visitors here?"

"No," she replied, "they all retired at eight o'clock."

Signers of the Declaration

Robert Treat Paine

1731–1814
Occupation – Lawyer
Wife – Sally Cobb
Children – 8
State – Massachusetts

Robert Treat Paine served as a chaplain during the French and Indian War and the American Revolution. He was trained for the ministry and served in that capacity for a time, but then became a lawyer. He was one of the prosecuting attorneys in the Boston Massacre trial of 1770. He once said, "I believe the Bible to be the written word of God and to contain in it the whole rule of faith and manners." At another time he said, "I desire to bless and praise the name of God most high for appointing me my birth in a land of Gospel Light, where the glorious tidings of a Savior and of pardon and salvation through Him have been continually sounding in mine ears."

Signers of the Declaration

William Paca

1740–1799
Occupation – Lawyer
Wives – Mary Chew
and Anne Harrison
Children – 6
State – Maryland

William Paca's estate was called Wye Hall. He, along with Charles Carroll and Samuel Chase, was in favor of independence. In 1782 he was elected as the governor of his native state. Toward the close of the war, he said, "We cannot pass over matters of so high concernment as religion and learning. The sufferings of the ministers of the gospel of all denominations, during the war, have been very considerable; and the perseverance and firmness of those, who discharged their sacred functions under many discouraging circumstances, claim our acknowledgments and thanks."

This was quite true so far as retiring went. Nothing was said about a subsequent rising.

"It is very strange," he remarked, musingly. "You were asleep, I know, for I knocked at your door three times before you heard me, yet it is certain that we were betrayed. I am altogether at a loss to conceive who could have given Washington information of our intended attack. But on arriving near his camp, we found him ready, with troops armed and cannon planted, prepared at all points to receive us. We have been compelled to turn on our heels and march back home again like a pack of fools."

As may well be surmised, the patriotic Lydia kept her own counsel, and not until the British had left Philadelphia was the important secret of that signal failure made known.

Burning Her House

By Celina Eliza Means, 1903

During the Revolution, the women distinguished themselves for their patriotism and courage as well as the men. One of the noted women of South Carolina was Mrs. Rebecca Motte. She was a wealthy widow of Orangeburg County. About the time of the surrender of Charleston, she had built a large house on her plantation. The mansion was an elegant one and occupied a commanding place on a high hill.

A British officer named McPherson took possession of Mrs. Motte's new mansion as a garrison for his soldiers. He was not brutal like Tarleton, but he thought it necessary to fortify himself in her house to protect himself against the Americans. He fortified the house by digging a ditch and making a high embankment around it. This fortified dwelling was the British Fort Motte.

Mrs. Motte was forced to move out of her new mansion, back into a smaller farmhouse which she had formerly occupied. McPherson politely helped her to move her household articles. In the house were a handsome bow and some arrows, brought from the East Indies some years before and given to Mrs. Motte's brother. These had been forgotten, but her niece, Mrs. Brewton, remembered them and went back into the mansion for them. Near the gate, she dropped one of the arrows out of the quiver. McPherson picked it up and was about to feel the point of it with his finger. "Stop, Lieutenant McPherson," said Mrs. Brewton, "the arrows are poisoned, and it might cost your arm or your life if one should scratch you."

Colonels Henry Lee and Marion, learning of McPherson's garrison, determined to attack him before Lord Rawdon, the British commander, could come to his aid. They soon found, however, that their small cannon could not dislodge him, and that the only chance to make him surrender was to burn the house.

To burn Mrs. Motte's mansion was a bitter trial to Colonel Lee. He had made her farmhouse his headquarters at her own invitation, and she had shown every manner of kindness and hospitality to him and his men. She had aided the needy soldiers and had visited the sick and wounded in camp. How could he tell her of his determination to burn the mansion? But before he announced to her his intention, she herself brought to him the East Indian bow and arrows and told him to tie burning cloth to the arrows and, with them, to shoot fire on the roof.

A strong-armed Scotchman was given the bow. He tied cloth soaked in turpentine to an arrow then lighted the cloth and shot it upon the roof of the house. It was hot, dry weather, and the shingles were soon in flames. McPherson ordered his men to climb up and put out the fire, but Captain Finley opened with his battery, raking the building from end to end. The fire was soon so hot that McPherson was forced to surrender.

After the surrender, the soldiers of both armies rushed in and extinguished the flames. Two years later, the mansion was accidentally burned.

Mrs. Motte had prepared dinner to which she asked both the American and British officers. When Lieutenant McPherson met Mrs. Brewton, he said, "You warned me of the poisoned arrow; it would have been a kindness to let me die rather than know the mortification of surrender."

Mrs. Motte turned to the young officer and said, "Lieutenant McPherson, it is not dishonor. Think of surrender as I did of the burning of my house, that it is one of the fortunes of war."

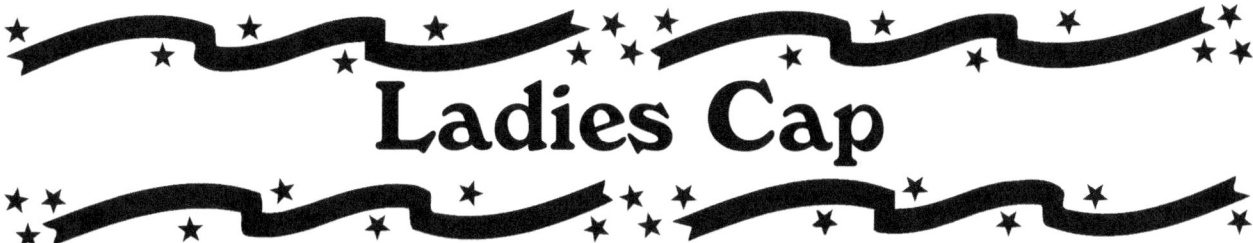

Ladies Cap

Women and girls of the American Revolution era nearly always wore some kind of cap or hat. Today we are going to make a simple cap similar to the ones worn by Revolutionary War ladies.

Cut a 25-inch square from white fabric. Hem all four sides by folding each side over ¼ of an inch and pressing, then fold it over another ¼ of an inch. Top stitch the hem. Top stitch lace to two edges. Fold into a triangle with the lace edges on the outside.

To wear, place on the head and tie under the chin.

If you have a large white or cream handkerchief, you could use that and just add lace to two edges. You could also look for a light colored scarf and cut it into a 25-inch square.

★★★★★★★★★★★★★★★★★★★★★★★★

"A patriot without religion in my estimation is as great a paradox as an honest man without the fear of God."
~Abigail Adams in a letter to Mercy Warren, 1775

★★★★★★★★★★★★★★★★★★★★★★★★

June 26

Putnam's Dashing Ride

By James Baldwin, 1916

It was early morning at East Greenwich, Connecticut. The sun had just risen, casting a golden glow over field and wood, and cheering the hearts of a little band of patriots who were breakfasting in a barnyard, while their horses, bridled and saddled, stood tied to the fence nearby. For this was in the year 1779, and the war for American Independence was at its height.

In the best room of the little farmhouse, General Israel Putnam was standing, his coat off, his shirtsleeves rolled up, his tanned cheeks whitened with a thick coat of lather. A razor was in his hand and, before him, hanging against the wall, was a cracked mirror. He was shaving. His beard was a week old and stubborn. The razor was dull, and the task he had undertaken proceeded but slowly.

He had just finished one rough cheek and was turning to the other when a flash of light in the looking-glass attracted his attention. It was like the reflection of the sunlight from some bright object outside of the open window behind him. What could it be? He paused in his shaving. The next moment, the flash was repeated, and he saw, distinctly pictured in the glass, a company of redcoat soldiers riding up over the hill crest behind him, not half a mile away.

He dropped his razor and, half-shaved, half-dressed, ran to the door and gave the alarm. Then, with the lather still whitening half of his face, he buckled his sword belt about him and hastily donned his threadbare coat and shapeless hat. Within a single brief minute, he was out of the house, had mounted his horse, and had put himself at the head of his little band. The patriots, so suddenly called from their breakfast, were already mounted and had ranged themselves in order across the road.

And now the redcoats were in plain sight. They were riding briskly and in order down the slope of the hill, apparently not aware of the near presence of an enemy.

"How many are they, Captain?" asked Putnam of his first officer.

"Fifteen hundred at the least," answered the captain.

"And how many have we here to oppose them?"

"Scarcely a hundred, Sir, scarcely a hundred."

"Then give them one volley, and let each man save himself if he can," commanded Putnam.

The redcoats drew rapidly nearer. The patriots raised their muskets. "Ready! Fire!" There was much noise and smoke, but the distance was too great, and nobody was hurt. Instantly the patriots wheeled their horses about and were away, pursued by the whole band of redcoats. Some

Thomas Stone

1743–1787
Occupation – Lawyer
Wife – Margaret Brown
Children – 3
State – Maryland

Thomas Stone had been so eager for an education that he willingly rode ten miles one way to go to school. His estate was called Habre-de-Venture. He was sent to Congress to keep the other three from voting for independence without the consent of the people. The people of Maryland told him, "We instruct you, that you do not, without the previous knowledge and approbation (approval) of the convention of this province, assent to any proposition to declare these colonies independent of the crown of Great Britain." When it came time to declare their freedom, Maryland had changed its mind, and Stone was glad to sign the document. In 1776, while serving in Congress, his wife Margaret Brown visited him in Philadelphia. Smallpox was common in that city and, as a precautionary action, she was inoculated against the smallpox. Her health went downhill after that and on June 1, 1787 she died. The heartbroken man died a short time afterward.

Signers of the Declaration

George Walton

1741–1804
Occupation – Lawyer
Wife – Dorothy Camber
Children – 2
State – Georgia

George Walton was apprenticed to a carpenter but later became a lawyer. While serving as a colonel in the Georgia militia, he was wounded and captured by the British during the siege of Savannah in 1778. He was a prisoner for nearly a year. In September of 1779 he was exchanged. He later served as a U.S. senator.

John Morton

1724–1777
Occupation – Farmer
Wife – Ann Justis
Children – 8
State – Pennsylvania

John Morton was the first signer to die. He died in the spring of 1777 of natural causes. After his death, his family had to flee from their home. Their farm was plundered by the British. The delegates of Pennsylvania were tied in their vote. He gave the deciding vote for independence. His will said, "With an awful reverence to the Great Almighty God, Creator of all mankind, being sick and weak in body but of sound mind and memory, thanks be given to Almighty God for the same."

---

took to the fields, some to the woods, and some, leaping from their horses, hid themselves in the nearby swamps. But General Putnam kept bravely to the road and galloped swiftly toward Stamford, with the best riders among the redcoats following close behind.

Over hills and through valleys and across streams the chase continued. The pursuers gained slowly but surely upon the pursued. Just north of Stamford, the road turned to the left, making a broad sweep around a hill. Just over the summit was a church and beyond it were some stone steps leading down to a pathway and another road. Here General Putnam suddenly wheeled his horse and leaving the highway, rode with unslackened speed up the steep slope of the hill, making a zigzag course until he reached the church.

In another moment, he had reached the stone steps. Down, down, the brave horse leaped with mighty strides, not once losing his foothold. The bottom was reached, the way was now clear, and the daring horseman was safe. When the redcoats came up and saw the perilous descent, not one of them had the courage to follow. They paused a few moments at the top of the stairway and then rode back to tell their companions of Putnam's daring ride.

"The Second Day of July 1776, will be the most memorable Epocha in the History of America. I am apt to believe that it will be celebrated, by succeeding Generations, as the great anniversary Festival. It ought to be commemorated, as the Day of Deliverance by solemn Acts of Devotion to God Almighty. It ought to be solemnized with Pomp and Parade, with Shows, Games, Sports, Guns, Bells, Bonfires, and Illuminations from one End of this Continent to the other from this Time forward forever more. You will think me transported with Enthusiasm but I am not. I am well aware of the Toil and Blood and Treasure, that it will cost Us to maintain this Declaration, and support and defend these States. Yet through all the Gloom I can see the Rays of ravishing Light and Glory. I can see that the End is more than worth all the Means. And that Posterity will triumph in that Days Transaction, even although We should rue it, which I trust in God We shall not."
- John Adams July 3, 1776

(Unfortunately Adams was mistaken. July 4 became the important date to remember and celebrate.)

Find the Cards

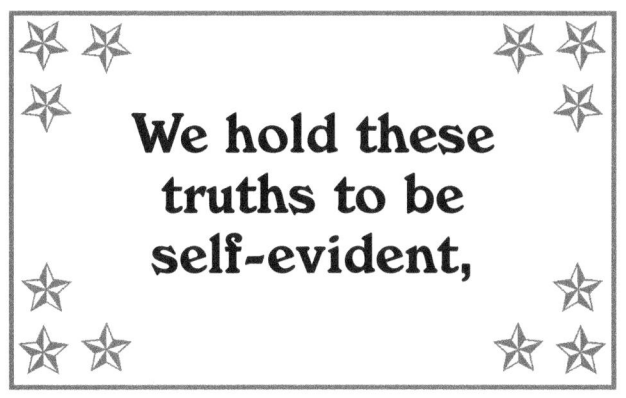

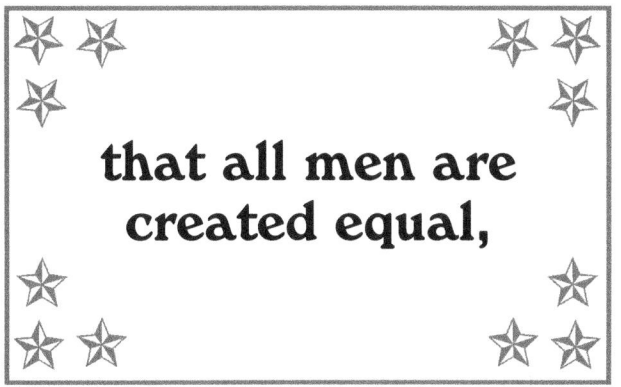

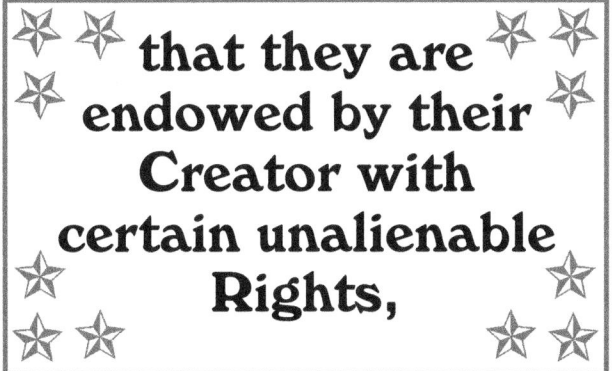

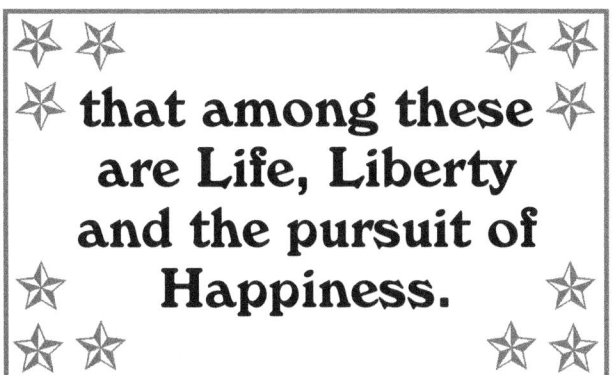

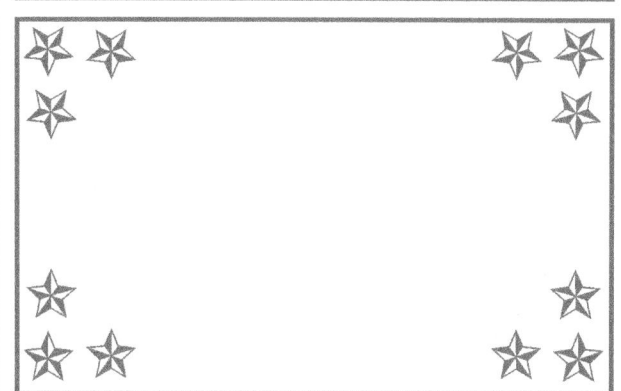

Print up the cards on this page and have one person hide them around the house or in the yard (if they are to be hidden outside, it would be a good idea to laminate them with clear contact paper). Once all four cards have been found, they must be put in the right order.

If there are enough players there might be several different teams. The cards for one team might be printed on blue paper, another might be on red paper, and a third might be on white paper. Each team can only pick up the cards that are their color. If they find a different colored card, they must leave it undisturbed.

Instead of teams, each individual person could have a specific color that he or she has to find.

The person or team who finds all the cards and puts them in the correct order wins!

You may use the blank ones below to add your own quote or poem.

Summer Countdown — Amy Puetz

June 27

Emily Geiger's Ride

By Benson John Lossing, 1889

On a mild, hazy day, in January of 1849, I was in Orangeburg, South Carolina, about eighty miles west of Charleston. My purpose was to visit the battleground of Eutaw Spring. I hired a horse and a gig for the journey.

At sunset I had traveled thirty miles. I lodged at the house of a planter some distance from Vance's Ferry on the Santee, where I passed the evening with an intelligent and respectable woman, Mrs. Buxton, who was eighty-four years of age. She was a maiden of seventeen when the armies of Greene and Rawdon made lively times in the American Revolution. She knew Marion and Sumter and other less famous partisan leaders, who were frequently at her father's house on the verge of a swamp, not far from the high hills of Santee.

"We were Whigs," she said, "but the Tories were so thick and cruel around us when Rawdon was at Camden that father had to pretend to be a king's man to save his life and property. Oh, those terrible times, when one was not sure on going to bed that the house would not be burned before morning!"

"Did you witness any exciting scenes yourself?" I inquired.

"Yes, many. One in particular so stirred my young blood that I actually resolved to put on brother Ben's clothes, take our old fowling-piece, join the Swamp Fox (as the British called Marion), and fight for freedom to call my soul my own."

"What was that event?" I asked.

"You have read, maybe," said Mrs. Buxton, "how Lord Rawdon, after chasing General Greene far toward the Saluda, suddenly turned back, abandoned Fort Ninety-six, and retreated toward Charleston. Well, Greene sent Harry Lee with his light-horse to get in front of Rawdon before he should reach the ferry on the Congaree River at Camden. He was anxious to call Marion and Sumter to the same point to help Lee. Sumter was then encamped a dozen miles south of our home."

The venerable woman's dark brown eyes sparkled with emotion as she proceeded with the story. She said her cousin, who was on Greene's staff at the time, told her that when the general called for a volunteer messenger to carry a letter to Sumter, not one of the soldiers offered to undertake the perilous task, for the way was swarming with Tories. Greene was perplexed. Brave and pretty Emily Geiger, the young daughter of a German planter in Fairfield District, had just arrived at headquarters with

Thomas McKean

1734–1817
Occupation – Lawyer
Wives – Mary Borden
and Sarah Armitage
Children – 11
State – Delaware

Thomas McKean signed the Articles of Confederation, served as the governor of Delaware, and was hunted by the British. He was in favor of independence. When George Read planned to vote no, this signer sent an urgent message to Caesar Rodney to come and break the tie. He had to move his family several times to escape being captured. He served in congress for many years. One of his most important contributions was being on the committee that watched the progress of Robert Aitken's printing of 10,000 Bibles for the use of schools, church, and families. He served as the president of congress in 1781 when he issued a thanksgiving proclamation that said, "Whereas it hath pleased Almighty God, the Father of Mercies, remarkably to assist and support the United States of America in their important struggle for liberty against the long–continued efforts of a powerful nation, it is the duty of all ranks to observe and thankfully acknowledge the interpositions of His Providence in their behalf."

Signers of the Declaration

Richard Stockton

1730–1781
Occupation – Lawyer
Wife – Annis Boudinot
Children – 6
State – New Jersey

Richard Stockton once said, "That the way of life held up in the Christian system is calculated for the most complete happiness that can be enjoyed in this mortal state." Richard Stockton married Annis Boudinot who was a noted poet and was called the Duchess of Morven. He and Benjamin Rush traveled to Scotland in 1766 to try and convince John Witherspoon to come to America and become the president of College of New Jersey (now called Princeton). The British pillaged and burned part of his estate (called Morven). In 1776 he left congress to move his family to safety. A Tory told the British where he was, and he was arrested and imprisoned. He was released the next year but his health was broken and he died in 1781. His daughter Julia married Benjamin Rush. In the will of this man who died prematurely from his captivity by the British he said, "As my children will have frequent occasion of perusing this instrument, and may probably be particularly impressed with the last words of their father, I think it proper here . . . to subscribe to the entire belief of the great and leading doctrines of the Christian religion."

important information for the general. She rode a spirited horse with the ease and grace of a dragoon. Emily, aware of the hesitation of the soldiers and Greene's anxiety, earnestly said to the general, "May I carry the letter?"

Greene was astonished. He was unwilling to expose her to the dangers which he knew awaited any messenger, for the Tories were vigilant.

"They won't hurt a young girl, I am sure, and I know the way," said Emily.

Greene's need was great, and he accepted her offer but with many misgivings. Fearing Emily might lose the letter on the way; he informed her of its contents, that she might deliver the message orally. She mounted her fleet horse with the general's blessing, and cheered by the admiring officers, she rode off at a brisk gallop. She crossed the Wateree River at Camden Ferry and pressed on toward the high hills of Santee.

Emily was riding at a rapid pace through an open, dry swamp when one of the Tory scouts, who was on the watch, confronted her with a gleaming bayonet. She reined up her steed.

Seizing her bridle, he exclaimed in excited tones, before noticing her face, "You are my prisoner!"

With perfect composure and in a firm voice she asked, "By whose authority am I detained?"

The scout was a tall young man, with long flaxen hair flowing from beneath a fashionable hat. He was confounded by the appearance and manner of his prisoner. They had observed a woman riding in haste from the direction of Greene's army toward the camp of Sumter and suspected her errand. She proved to be a young maiden, fair as a lily, with mild blue eyes and a profusion of brown hair. The young scout, smitten with her beauty and air of innocence, released his hold upon the bridle, when an older companion, made of sterner stuff, seized the reins and led the horse to an unoccupied house on the edge of a swamp and bade her dismount. The younger soldier gallantly assisted her to alight, and she was taken into the house. With proper delicacy, the scouts sent for Mrs. Buxton's mother, living a mile distant, to search Emily's clothing.

"I went with mother," said Mrs. Buxton, "to see a woman prisoner. The door of the house was guarded by the younger scout, who was Peter Simons, son of a neighbor two miles away, and a right gallant young fellow he was. After the war, he married my sister."

"Then you saw the young prisoner?" I asked. "Yes, and I helped mother search her. We were amazed when we saw, instead of a haughty middle-aged woman, as we supposed a spy must be, a sweet young girl about my own age, looking as innocent as a pigeon.

"Our sympathies were with her, but Mother performed her duty faithfully. We found nothing on her person that would afford a suspicion that she was a spy. She was released by the scouts, who offered her many apologies for detaining her. She had been too smart for them. While alone in the house guarded by Peter Simons, she had eaten up Greene's letter piece by piece. So, secure from detection, she willingly submitted to our search and told us frankly who she was."

"'My name is Geiger—Emily Geiger,' she said. 'My father is a planter near Winnsboro, in Fairfield, and I am on my way to visit friends below.'

"Wasn't she smart?" said the old lady. "She was going to 'visit friends below'—Sumter and his men—our friends likewise, for that matter. When the scouts dismissed her, we took her to our house, gave her some refreshments, and urged her to stay with us until morning. But she could not be persuaded, saying the two armies were so near it might soon become impossible to reach her friends. Peter Simons had accompanied us home and offered to escort Emily to her friends as a protector. She declined his offer and rode away, bearing our silent blessings. We saw no more of her until after the war."

"Did she reach Sumter's camp in safety?" I inquired.

"Yes, and delivered Greene's message word for word as he had written it."

Sumter and Marion joined forces and hastened to Friday's Ferry at Granby. Rawdon, baffled, did not attempt to cross the Congaree, but fled before the pursuing Americans toward Orangeburg, on the Edisto.

"You say you saw no more of Emily Geiger until some time after the war," I remarked. "What was her fate?"

"A happy one. She had married a rich young planter on the Congaree, named John Threwits. Soon after the close of the war, Emily and her husband, returning from a visit with her parents in Fairfield, went out of their way to revisit the scene of her perilous exploit. They had crossed the Wateree at Camden Ferry as she had done before, visited the house in which she had been searched, and rode to our home to thank my mother for her kindness on that occasion. They had with them a sweet little baby a few months old. Peter Simons was then my sister's husband and at our house. Emily stood face to face with her jailer for an hour. She freely told her story and owned that

John Witherspoon

1723–1794
Occupation – Minister
Wives – Elizabeth Montgomery
and Mrs. Ann Dill
Children – 12
State – New Jersey

John Witherspoon thought that America was "not only ripe for the measure (the Declaration) but in danger of rotting for the want of it." He used his position as the president of Princeton to encourage independence. The British burned many of the buildings in retaliation for his actions. He once said, "Pure democracy cannot subsist long nor be carried far into the departments of state. It is very subject to caprice and the madness of popular rage." He was on the committee that commissioned the printing of 10,000 Bibles by Robert Aitken. He lost his son, James, in the American Revolution. He once said, "God grant that, in America, true religion and civil liberty may be inseparable and that the unjust attempts to destroy the one may, in the issue, tend to the support and establishment of both." At another time he said, "He is the best friend to American liberty who is the most sincere and active in promoting true and undefiled religion, and who sets himself with the greatest firmness to bear down profanity and immorality of every kind. Whoever is an avowed enemy of God, I scruple not to call him an enemy to his country."

Signers of the Declaration

Charles Carroll

1737–1832
Occupation – Planter
Wife – Mary Darnall
Children – 7
State – Maryland

Charles Carroll was the only Roman Catholic signer, and he was the last signer to die. He added "of Carrollton" after his name to distinguish himself from several other members of his family who had the same name. He had an estate called Carrollton Manor, but he spent most of his time at Doughoregan Manor. He was thought to be the wealthiest signer.

William Whipple

1730–1785
Occupation – Merchant
Wife – Catherine Moffat
Children – 1 (died young)
State – New Hampshire

William Whipple went to sea at a young age and became a captain and eventually a merchant. He was a brigadier-general for the New Hampshire militia and helped win the victory at Saratoga in 1777.

---

she was much startled when Peter seized her bridle, but she controlled her feelings. She told us of her dinner on Greene's dispatch and thought how silly the young scout was in leaving her alone in the house while he guarded the door on the outside. Peter wasn't much of a Tory, and we all rejoiced that a kind Providence had protected Emily from detection.

"The ways of God are mysterious," said the elderly lady, laying her hand on my knee. "Peter's son married Emily's daughter—the sweet little baby she brought to our house—and their son owns a plantation a few miles from here."

It is said that General Greene gave her a pair of earrings and a brooch and, in 1825, when General Lafayette visited the United States, he gave her a beautiful silk shawl.

American Revolution Quiz

See how much you know about the American Revolution. Answers are below.

1. Who was the most famous U.S. general of the war?
2. Finish the sentence. Yankee Doodle keep it up, Yankee doodle dandy. Mind the music and the . . .
3. Who was the famous founding father who had many witty sayings, such as, "People who are wrapped up in themselves make small packages."
4. Who was the famous Frenchman who fought for America?
5. This brave woman took her husbands place firing a cannon when he was injured.
6. What famous bell hangs in Independence Hall?
7. Who was the leader of the Green Mountain Boys that captured Fort Ticonderoga, "In the name of the Great Jehovah and the Continental Congress."?
8. Where did Cornwallis surrender?

Answers
1. George Washington
2. Step, and with the girls be handy.
3. Benjamin Franklin
4. Marquis de Lafayette
5. Molly Pitcher
6. The Liberty Bell
7. Ethan Allen
8. Yorktown

June 28

John Paul Jones
By Albert Blaisdell, 1922

On the fourteenth of June 1777, the Continental Congress voted, "That the flag of the thirteen United States be thirteen stripes, alternate red and white; that the union be thirteen stars, white in a blue field, representing a new constellation."

Soon after this, General Washington, Robert Morris, and George Ross called on Betsy Ross, a seamstress in Philadelphia. She was noted for her fine needlework, and they wished her to make a sample flag for the nation. She made such a beautiful flag that she was engaged to make all the flags used by the government. The little brick house in Arch Street, where she lived and made the flags, is still standing. Many people visit this spot every year.

The national flag is called the Stars and Stripes. It is sometimes called Old Glory.

The Stars and Stripes was raised for the first time on the third of August 1777. This was a rude flag made hastily out of a white shirt, a blue jacket, and a red petticoat. It was raised at Fort Stanwix in New York.

It is said that the first Stars and Stripes used in the navy was raised by John Paul Jones.

On the same day that the Continental Congress voted to have a new flag for the new nation, it passed the following resolution also: "Resolved that Captain John Paul Jones be appointed to the ship *Ranger*."

"The flag and I are twins; we were born on the same day," said the young officer.

John Paul Jones was born in Scotland. He was the son of a poor gardener. From earliest childhood, he loved the water. When only twelve years old, he went to sea.

He began his service to the United States as an officer on the *Alfred*, the flagship of our little navy. It is said that on this vessel he raised, with his own hand, the original flag of the Revolution. This was the pine tree flag.

John Paul Jones was soon made a captain.

When he came to Portsmouth in New Hampshire, to take command of the little warship *Ranger*, he found that she had no flag.

"This will never do," he said. "Of course the *Ranger* must have the new flag."

Now it seems that a group of girls in Portsmouth were planning to have a quilting party. Captain Jones was invited to the party.

"I am under orders to sail in a few days," he said to the young women. "The *Ranger* must have a flag. I am going to fight on the high seas. Will you help me?"

"Yes, indeed, Captain Jones," answered Patience Bartlett, a leader among the girls. "We will do our best to help you. We have heard of your brave deeds along

John Hancock

1737–1793
Occupation – Merchant
Wife – Dorothy Quincy
Children – 2
State – Massachusetts

He also signed the Articles of Confederation and served as the governor of Massachusetts. He was one of the richest men in New England. As the president of the convention, he was the first man to sign the Declaration of Independence. He signed his name in a bold, big, clear hand and is reported to have said, "I write so plain that George the Third may read without his spectacles. And he can double the reward on my head." Hancock and the secretary of the convention, Charles Thomson, were the only two signatures of the first copy of the Declaration that was presented to the public. On August 2, 1776, an official copy with the delegates' signature was signed.

the coast. You have won the personal regard of General Washington himself."

These Portsmouth girls were much in earnest and very patriotic. As the story is told, they made the flag from their best silk gowns—red, white, and blue. When the flag was finished, they went to the ship to present it to the gallant young captain.

"Hip, hip, hurrah!" they shouted as the flag was raised to the breeze.

On the first day of November, with the silk flag flying at her masthead, the *Ranger* sailed for the coast of Great Britain.

Captain Jones was anxious to see how his ship would behave when she met a British man-of-war. He soon found out. In the summer of 1778, she had a fight with the *Drake*, a British sloop-of-war. For the first time, a British warship lowered her flag to the Stars and Stripes.

Captain Jones' exploits abroad won him great renown in the United States. He was put in command of a much larger ship, furnished by the French government. The name of this ship he changed to *Bon Homme Richard*, in honor of Benjamin Franklin who had written *Poor Richard's Almanac*. The same silk flag was waving in the breeze.

In August of 1779, the famous battle took place between the *Bon Homme Richard* and the British frigate *Serapis*.

This was one of the most desperate sea fights ever known in naval history. After fighting for a long time, the British captain asked Jones if he was ready to surrender.

John Paul Jones replied, "I have not yet begun to fight."

It ended in the surrender of the *Serapis*, but the *Bon Homme Richard* was a wreck. Captain Jones left her and took his men on board the British warship. The next day his gallant old vessel sank, carrying with her the Portsmouth flag. For this victory, Captain Jones was honored in France and at home.

In due time, he came back to America. He met one of the young women who had helped to make his silk flag.

"My dear young lady," he said, "I longed to bring back home to you the beautiful flag you gave me four years ago, but I could not bear to take it from the sinking ship."

In his diary, the gallant hero of twenty-four naval battles described the last moments of the *Bon Homme Richard* and her little silk flag that had never known defeat: "No one was now left aboard the *Richard* but her dead. To them I gave the good old ship for their coffin. In her they

Signers of the Declaration

Abraham Clark

1726–1794
Occupation – Lawyer and Farmer
Wife – Sarah Hatfield
Children – 10
State – New Jersey

Abraham Clark was the only child of a farmer, but poor health kept him from personally working the land. Instead he taught himself how to be a lawyer. He once said, "Perhaps our Congress will be exalted on a high Gallows." He had two sons who were captured by the British. They were kept on the dreaded prison ship *Jersey* until finally exchanged. He was elected to the Constitutional Convention, but poor health prevented him from attending. He opposed the Constitution without a Bill of Rights. He served in the U.S. House of Representatives after the adoption of the Constitution.

George Taylor

1716–1781
Occupation – Ironmaster
Wife – Anne Savage
Children – 2
State – Pennsylvania

George Taylor came to America as an indentured servant and was the only ironmaster to sign the Declaration. He used his skill with iron to make grapeshot, cannonballs, and cannons for the Continental army.

found a sublime burial place. She rolled heavily in the long swell, settled slowly by the head, and sank peacefully in about forty fathoms. Our torn and tattered flag was left flying when we left her. As she plunged down by the head, at the last, the rail across the stern rose in the air; so the very last thing mortal eyes ever saw of the *Bon Homme Richard* was the defiant waving of her unconquered and unstricken flag as she went down."

Cocked Hat

John Paul Jones (pictured at right) wore a cocked hat.

To make a cocked hat, you will need a sheet of newspaper. Any size paper may be used, but it works best if the sheet is at least 13½ inches wide.

Take a piece of newspaper and fold according to the instructions below.

1. Fold along the line A B, doubling the paper (FIG. 1).
2. Fold along the lines C D and C E (FIG. 1).
3. Fold the top layer along F G and then again at D E (FIG. 1).
4. Turn the hat over, so the bottom is on top (FIG. 2). Fold the edges toward the inside about ½ an inch lines H I and J K (FIG. 3).
5. Fold along the L M line (FIG. 3).
6. Fold up along the N O line (FIG. 3).
7. Tape the edges shut. Tape or glue a feather to finish it.
8. The hat may be painted with craft paint to cover up the writing, or you may use a brown paper bag or newsprint instead of a newspaper.

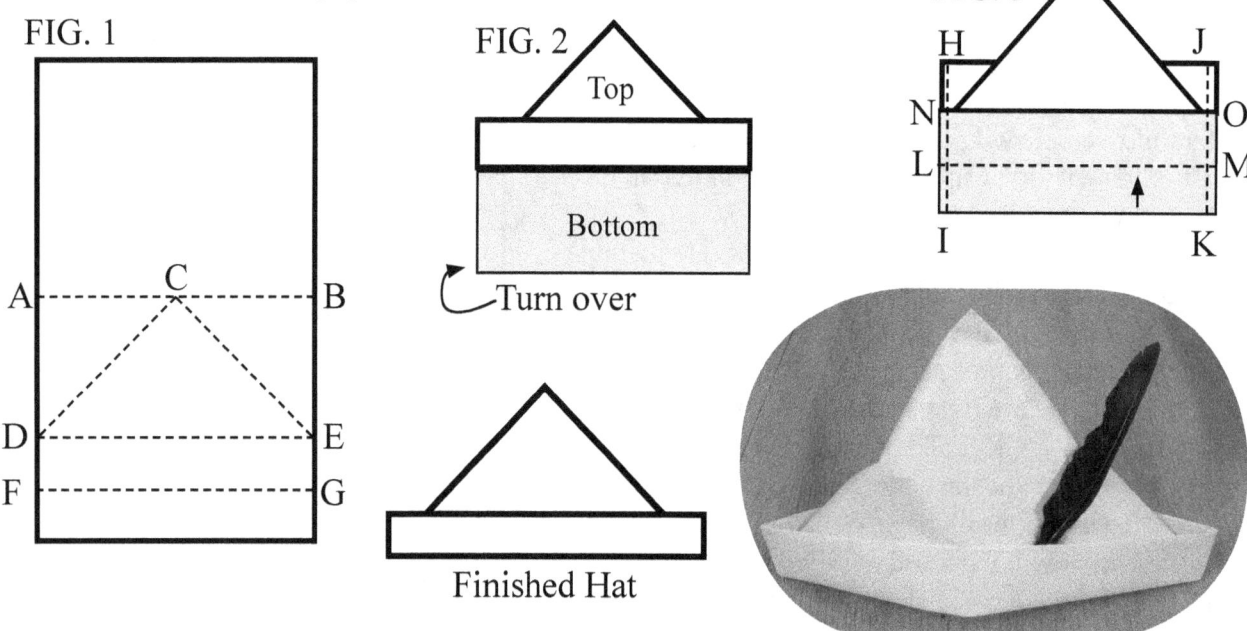

Summer Countdown   **Amy Puetz**

June 29

Gold in the Bread
By Albert Blaisdell, 1922

It was in August in the year 1780. Affairs had gone from bad to worse in the South. The British overran South Carolina and Georgia. Cornwallis, the British commander, ordered Tarleton and Ferguson to enlist soldiers among the Tories.

At this time, there lived in North Carolina, on a plantation, Richard and Abigail Merrill. They had three children. Polly was sixteen years old, Abigail fourteen, and Peter about three.

Mr. and Mrs. Merrill were just starting on horseback to do a bit of business a few miles from their home.

"Take good care of Peter," said Mr. Merrill to Abigail. "See that he does not get into trouble. I'm sure there are no Tories to do you any harm."

"And Polly dear," said Mrs. Merrill, "about ten o'clock, don't forget to bake the bread."

Off rode the father and mother, leaving the three children alone. The trip was short, and they expected to get back before night.

The girls were busy at work. Polly made the bread while Abigail was playing with Peter on the front porch.

Suddenly Abigail came running into the house with Peter in her arms.

"Oh, Polly!" she said, "just look out the front window. Down by the river road I saw some men riding this way. I'm sure they are Tories. What shall we do?"

The girls knew that their father had been paid some money a few days before, and that the pieces of gold had been put in a big wallet and locked up in a bureau drawer.

In a few moments, the tramp of horses' feet and the sharp order of an officer were heard. A band of Tories came riding up the hill near the house.

"Run quick, Abigail," cried Polly, "get the key to the bureau and bring me the wallet. I'll hide it somewhere."

It took only a moment for Abigail to unlock the bureau drawer and bring the wallet to Polly.

"I know what I'll do," said Polly, as she took a quick look at the bread ready for the oven. "Perhaps I can save the money. I'll try it."

Quick as a flash she put a little dough into a pan, and poured in the pieces of gold. She then covered the money with dough and pushed the pan into the brick oven.

"You have done it this time," laughed Abigail. "Not even a Tory will look in there for money."

"Don't be too sure, Abigail. Hurry now. Put the wallet back in the bureau drawer, and then go out on the porch and play with Peter."

Captain Mott took off his hat and bowed politely to the girls.

"Don't be afraid, girls. We met your father down the road. He told us to stop here and get the money which he received last week. He told us where he kept it. Be quick and get it for us, for we must hurry along."

Polly kept cool and stood her ground.

Signers of the Declaration

Elbridge Gerry

1744–1814
Occupation – Merchant
Wife – Ann Thompson
Children – 10
State – Massachusetts

Elbridge Gerry signed the Articles of Confederation, was sent to the Constitutional Convention, served as the governor of Massachusetts, and was the vice president from 1813–14. As a member of the council of safety for Massachusetts, he was attending a meeting in between Cambridge and Lexington when the British marched to Lexington. He was nearly captured by the English but managed to escape just in time. He helped alter the lines of a voting district to help win the vote. The line was curvy like a salamander and his opponents called it "gerrymander" after him. Elbridge Gerry's wife was the last wife of the signers to die. She died in 1849. Elbridge Gerry's daughter, Emily Louise, was the last signer's child to die. She died in 1894.

"My father would never give you the money, and I'm sure I shall not."

"Then I will look for it until I find it."

With some angry words, Captain Mott stepped into the bedroom and began to ransack the bureau drawers.

In her haste, Abigail had left the wallet in plain sight. When Captain Mott seized it, two or three coins rolled out and fell on the floor.

Peter had followed them into the room. He ran and picked up the pieces of gold and gave them to the officer.

"Pretty money," said the little boy. "More in fower."

Polly's heart beat fast as she listened to her little brother's childish talk.

"He must have seen me hide the gold in the pan of dough. The secret is out. The Tories will surely find the money."

Captain Mott laughed. "Good enough, my little boy. Children and fools tell the truth. Come with me and show me where your father buried the pretty money in the flowers."

Peter took the officer's hand and led the way into the flower garden.

The officer set his men to digging up the shrubs and rose bushes.

With her eyes as big as saucers, Polly watched the men digging in the garden. Suddenly she knew what Peter meant. A few days before, a pet rabbit of the family had died, and the girls had buried it in a box in the garden.

After a while, one of the soldiers struck his shovel against something hard. With a shout, he pulled from the ground the box that held the rabbit's dead body.

"You have done well," cried Captain Mott. "Bring that box to me."

In another moment, one of the officers rode in great haste into the yard shouting, "To horse, to horse! Marion's men are after us not a mile away."

A few minutes more, and Captain Mott and his Tories were riding away as fast as they could go.

Polly laughed until she cried.

"They will surely come back as soon as they find they have been made fools of. Let me think what I can do."

She fastened the door with the oak bar. She took down her father's long rifle. She was now ready to fight.

Suddenly there was a clatter of horses' shoes on the rocky road.

"Hello, neighbor Merrill, open the door and let us in," somebody shouted.

Signers of the Declaration

Lyman Hall

1724–1790
Occupation – Physician and Minister
Wives – Abigail Burr and Mary Osburn
Children – 1
State – Georgia

Lyman Hall had an estate called Hall's Knoll. Originally educated as a theologian, he later became a doctor. The colony of Georgia did not feel the need for independence as much as the other colonies. However, he wanted to join the other colonies in revolting. He even went so far as to suggest that his county should separate from Georgia so they could join the cause of freedom. The British destroyed his home during the Revolution. He served as the governor of Georgia.

George Ross

1730–1779
Occupation – Lawyer
Wife – Anne Lawler
Children – 3
State – Pennsylvania

He represented Pennsylvania at the first Continental Congress in 1774. He was a peacemaker who helped to negotiate a treaty with the Indians and provide justice for Tories. He was educated by his father who was a minister in the Episcopal Church. His sister Gertrude Ross married fellow signer George Read.

Signers of the Declaration

Josiah Bartlett

1729–1795
Occupation – Physician
Wife – Mary Bartlett
Children – 12
State – New Hampshire

After the president of the congress signed the Declaration, Josiah Bartlett was the next to sign. He was the first governor of New Hampshire after the states agreed to the Constitution.

George Clymer

1739–1813
Occupation – Merchant
Wife – Elizabeth Meredith
Children – 9
State – Pennsylvania

As a wealthy merchant, George Clymer first became interested in independence because of the restrictions Britain put on trade. After the British victory at Brandywine, Pennsylvania in 1777, the British troops plundered George Clymer's home in Chester County. His wife and children escaped and hid in the woods. He financially helped the country by exchanging all his money for Continental currency. He also signed the Constitution and served as a representative from Pennsylvania in the first U.S. Congress.

Laughing and crying by turns, the two girls opened the door to a party of sturdy patriots.

"You are brave and sensible girls," said the leader. "You outwitted the rascals. They won't come back. They did not want to fight. They only wanted to steal."

What a merry time it was that evening when Mr. and Mrs. Merrill came home!

"I burned the bread," said Polly, "but the money is safe."

Star Sandwiches

Use a star-shaped cookie cutter to cut a star shape in one slice of bread. On the other slice of bread, spread the peanut butter and strawberry jam (blueberry may also be used). Put the slice with the star cut on top of the other piece. The sandwich may be served like that, or the cut-out star may be reinserted. You might also take the cut star and put a little butter and cinnamon on it and then put it in the broiler until golden brown.

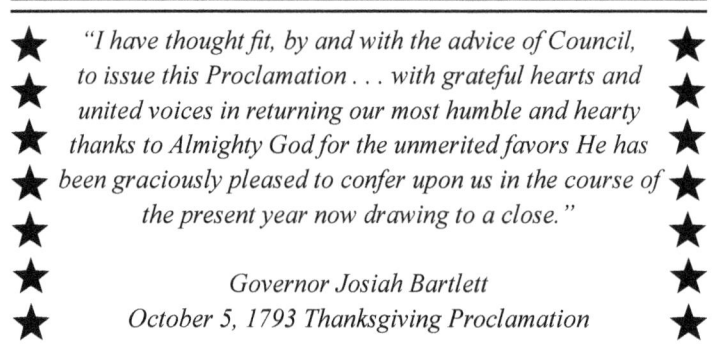

"I have thought fit, by and with the advice of Council, to issue this Proclamation . . . with grateful hearts and united voices in returning our most humble and hearty thanks to Almighty God for the unmerited favors He has been graciously pleased to confer upon us in the course of the present year now drawing to a close."

Governor Josiah Bartlett
October 5, 1793 Thanksgiving Proclamation

June 30

On the Track of a Traitor

By Charles Morris, 1895

While Major Andre was dying the death of a spy; General Benedict Arnold was living the life of a cherished traitor in the midst of the British army at New York. This was a state of affairs far from satisfactory to the American authorities. The messenger had been captured while the mastermind behind the scheme had escaped. Could Arnold be captured and made to pay the penalty of his treason, it would be a good lesson to any who might feel disposed to follow his dishonorable example.

Washington had his secret correspondents in New York, and from them had learned that Arnold was living in quarters adjoining those of Sir Henry Clinton, at but a short distance from the river and apparently with no thought of or precaution against danger. It might be possible to seize him and carry him away bodily from the midst of his new friends.

Sending for Major Henry Lee, a brave and shrewd cavalry leader, Washington broached to him this important matter and submitted a plan of action which seemed to him to promise success.

"It is a delicate and dangerous project," he said. "Much depends on our finding an agent fit for such hazardous work. You may have the man in your corps. Whoever volunteers for this duty will lay me under the greatest personal obligation and may expect an ample reward. But no time is to be lost. He must proceed if possible, tonight."

"Not only courage and daring, but very peculiar talent is needed for such an enterprise," said Lee. "I have plenty of brave men, but can think of only one whom I can recommend for such a duty as this. His name is John Champe. His rank, sergeant-major, but there is one serious obstacle in the way. He must appear to desert, and I fear that Champe has too high a sense of military honor for that."

"Try him," said Washington. "The service he will do to his country far outweighs anything he can do in the ranks. Rumor says that other officers of high rank are ready to follow Arnold's example. If we can punish this traitor, he will have no imitators."

"I can try," answered Lee. "I may succeed. Champe is not without ambition, and the object to be attained is a great one. I may safely promise him the promotion which he ardently desires."

"That will be but part of his reward," said Washington.

Lee sent for Champe. In response, a young man entered. He was large, muscular, serious, silent, and thoughtful. His words were few which made him safe to trust with a secret and his sense of honor high. In all the army, there was not his superior in courage and determination in anything he should undertake.

It was no agreeable surprise to the worthy fellow to learn what he was desired to do. The plan was an admirable

Signers of the Declaration

Benjamin Harrison

1726–1791
Occupation – Planter
Wife – Elizabeth Bassett
Children – 7
State – Virginia

Benjamin Harrison was a large man and, after signing the Declaration, remarked to the small Elbridge Gerry, "I shall have a great advantage over you, Mr. Gerry, when we are all hung for what we are now doing. From the size and weight of my body, I shall die in a few minutes, but from the lightness of your body, you will dance in the air an hour or two before you are dead." His estate was Berkeley. He was the speaker of the Virginia House of Delegates. His youngest son (William Henry Harrison) became the 9th president, his grandson Benjamin Harrison became the 23rd president.

one, he admitted; it promised the best results. He did not care for peril, and was ready to venture on anything that would not involve his honor; but to desert from his corps, to win the scorn and detestation of his fellows, to seem to play the traitor to his country—these were serious obstacles. He begged to be excused.

Lee combated his objections. Success promised honor to himself and to his corps, the gratitude of his country, the greatest service to his beloved commander in chief. Desertion, for such a purpose, carried with it no dishonor, and any stain upon his character would vanish when the truth became known. The conference was a long one. In the end Lee's arguments prevailed. Champe yielded and promised to undertake the mission.

The necessary instructions had already been prepared by Washington himself. The chosen agent was to deliver letters to two persons in New York who were in Washington's confidence and who would lend him their assistance. He was to use his own judgment in procuring aid for the capture of Arnold, and to lay such plans as circumstances should suggest, and he was strictly ordered not to kill the traitor under any circumstances.

All this settled, the question of the difficulties in the way arose. Between the American camp and the British outpost were many pickets and patrols. Parties of marauding patriots, like those that had seized Andre, might be in the way. Against these Lee could offer no aid. The desertion must seem a real one. All he could do would be to delay pursuit. For the rest, Champe must trust to his own skill and daring.

Eleven o'clock was the hour fixed. At that hour the worthy sergeant, taking his cloak, bag, and orderly-book, and with three guineas in his pocket, which Lee had given him, secretly mounted his horse and slipped quietly from the camp.

Lee immediately went to bed, pretending to sleep, though he had never been more awake. Half an hour passed. Then a heavy tread was heard outside the major's quarters, and a loud knock came upon his door. It was some time before he could be aroused.

"Who is there?" he asked, in sleepy tones.

"It is I—Captain Carnes," was the reply. "I am here for orders. One of our patrols has just fallen in with a dragoon who put spurs to his horse on being challenged, and fled at full speed. He is a deserter and must be pursued."

Lee still seemed half asleep. He questioned the officer in a drowsy way, affecting not to understand him. When at

Signers of the Declaration

Samuel Chase

1741–1811
Occupation – Lawyer
Wives – Ann Baldwin and Hannah Kilty Giles
Children – 8
State – Maryland

Samuel Chase was educated by his father, an Anglican minister. He was deeply concerned about independence. He, Charles Carroll, and William Paca convinced their state that separating from Great Britain would be the best thing for Maryland. In 1796 this delegate was made an associate judge of the Supreme Court by President Washington.

Francis Hopkinson

1737–1791
Occupation – Lawyer and Musician
Wife – Ann Borden
Children – 5
State – New Jersey

Francis Hopkinson's home was plundered by the British during the Revolution. His wife Ann had a sister named Mary, who was the wife of Thomas McKean. He wrote *A Political Catechism* in 1777.

length the captain's purpose was made clear to his seemingly drowsy wits, Lee ridiculed the idea that one of his men had deserted. Such a thing had happened but once during the whole war. He could not believe it possible.

"It has happened now," persisted Captain Carnes. "The fellow is a deserter and must be pursued."

Lee still affected disbelief and was with difficulty brought to order that the whole squadron should be mustered, to see if any of them were missing. This done; there was no longer room for doubt or delay. Champe, the sergeant-major, was gone, and with him his arms, baggage, and orderly-book.

Signers of the Declaration

Matthew Thornton

1714–1803
Occupation – Physician
Wife – Hannah Jack
Children – 5
State – New Hampshire

Matthew Thornton served as a surgeon during King George's War of the 1740s. He went with the British force that captured Louisbourg in Nova Scotia. He once said, "We would, therefore, recommend to the colony at large, to cultivate that Christian union, harmony, and tender affection, which is the only foundation upon which our invaluable privileges can rest with any security, or our public measures be pursued with the least prospect of success." Another time he said, "In a word, we seriously and earnestly recommend the practice of that pure and undefiled religion, which embalmed the memory of our pious ancestors, as that alone upon which we can build a solid hope and confidence in the Divine protection and favor, without whose blessing all the measures of safety we have, or can propose, will end in our shame and disappointment."

Captain Carnes ordered that pursuit should be made at once. Here, too, Lee made such delay as he could without arousing suspicion, and when the pursuing party was ready, he changed its command, giving it to Lieutenant Middleton, a tender-hearted young man whom he could trust to treat Champe mercifully if he should be overtaken. These various delays had the desired effect. By the time the party started, Champe had been an hour on the road.

It was past twelve o'clock of a starry night when Middleton and his men took to horse and galloped away on the track of the deserter. It was a plain track, unfortunately—a trail that a child might have followed. There had been a shower at sunset, sharp enough to wash out all previous hoof marks from the road. The footprints of a single horse were all that now appeared. In addition to this, the horseshoes of Lee's legion had a private mark by which they could be readily recognized. There could be no question; those footprints were made by the horse of the deserter.

Here was a difficulty unlooked for by Lee. The pursuit could be pushed on at full speed. At every fork or cross-road, a trooper sprang quickly from his horse and examined the trail. It needed but a glance to discover what road had been taken. On they went, with scarce a moment's loss of time, and with sure knowledge that they were on the fugitive's track.

At sunrise the pursuing party found themselves at the top of a ridge near the Three Pigeons, a roadside tavern several miles north of the village of Bergen. Looking ahead, their eyes fell on the form of the deserter. He was but half a mile in advance. They had gained on him greatly during the night.

At the same moment, Champe perceived them. Both parties spurred their horses to greater speed, and away went fugitive and pursuers at a rattling pace. The roads in that vicinity were well known to them all. There was a short-cut through the woods from near the Three Pigeons to the bridge below Bergen. Middleton sent part of his men by this route to cut off the fugitive, while he followed the main road with the rest. He felt sure now that he had the deserter, for he could not reach the British outposts without crossing the bridge.

On they went. No long time elapsed before the two divisions met at the bridge. But Champe was not between them. The trap had been sprung but had failed to catch its game. He had in some strange manner disappeared. What was to be done? How had he eluded them?

Middleton rode hastily back to Bergen and inquired if a dragoon had passed through the village that morning.

"Yes, and not long ago."

"Which way did he go?"

"That we cannot say. No one took notice."

Middleton examined the road. Other horses had been out that morning, and the Lee corps footprint was no longer to be seen. But at a short distance from the village, the trail again became legible and the pursuit was resumed. In a few minutes Champe was discovered. He had reached a point near the water's edge, and was making signals to certain British galleys which lay in the stream.

The truth was that the fugitive knew of the short-cut quite as well as his pursuers, and had shrewdly judged that they would take it and endeavor to cut him off before he could reach the enemy's lines at Paulus Hook. He knew, besides, that two of the king's galleys lay in the bay a mile from Bergen, and in front of the small settlement of Communipaw. There he hurried, throwing his bag upon his back, as his horse ran.

Champe now found himself in imminent peril of capture. There had been no response from the galleys to his signals. The pursuers were close at hand and pushing forward with shouts of triumph. Soon they were but a few hundred yards away. There was but one hope left. Champe sprang from his horse, flung away the scabbard of his sword, and with the naked blade in his hand, ran across the marshy ground before him, leaped into the waters of the bay, and swam quickly for the galleys, calling loudly for help.

A boat had just before left the side of the nearest galley. As the pursuers reined up their horses by the side of the marsh, the fugitive was hauled in and swiftly rowed back to the ship. Middleton, disappointed in his main object, took the horse, cloak, and scabbard of the fugitive and returned with them to camp.

"He has not been killed?" asked Lee, hastily, on seeing these articles.

"No, the rascal gave us the slip. He is safely on a British galley, and this is all we have to show."

A few days afterward, Lee received a letter from Champe, in a disguised hand and without signature, transmitted through a secret channel which had been arranged, telling of his success up to this point, and what he proposed to do.

As it appeared, the seeming deserter had been well received in New York. The sharpness of the pursuit and the orderly-book which he bore seemed satisfactory proofs of his sincerity of purpose. The captain of the galley sent him to New York with a letter to Sir Henry Clinton.

Clinton was glad to see him. For a deserter to come to him from a legion so faithful to the rebel cause as that of Major Lee seemed an evidence that the American side was rapidly weakening. He questioned Champe closely. The masquerading deserter answered him briefly, but with such a show of sincerity as to win his confidence. The interview ended in Clinton's giving him a couple of guineas, and bidding him to call on General Arnold, who was forming a corps of loyalists and deserters, and who would be glad to have his name on his rolls. This suggestion hit Champe's views exactly. It was what had been calculated upon by Washington in advance. Champe called upon Arnold, who received him courteously and gave him quarters among his recruiting sergeants. He asked him to join his legion, but Champe declined, saying that, if caught by the rebels in this corps, he was sure to be hanged.

Signers of the Declaration

Thomas Nelson Jr.

1738–1789
Occupation – Planter and Merchant
Wife – Lucy Grymes
Children – 13
State – Virginia

Thomas Nelson Jr. owned a house in Yorktown, and when he noticed that the American troops were not bombarding it, he ordered them to do so when he learned that the British were using it as their headquarters. He served in the Virginia House of Burgesses. He was the commander in chief of Virginia militia and often paid the militiamen under him out of his own pocket. He served as the governor of Virginia after Thomas Jefferson. He helped raise money for the army and promised to pay it back himself if the government did not.

In a few days, the secret agent had made his plans. He delivered the letters which had been given him, and made arrangements with one of the parties written to for aid in the proposed abduction of Arnold. This done, he went to Arnold, told him that he had changed his mind, and agreed to enlist in his legion. His purpose now was to gain free intercourse with him, that he might learn all that was possible about his habits.

Arnold's quarters were at Number Three Broadway. Behind the house was a garden which extended toward the water's edge. Champe soon learned that it was Arnold's habit to return to his quarters about midnight, and that before going to bed he always visited the garden. Adjoining this garden was a dark alley which led to the street. In short, all the surroundings and circumstances were adapted to the design and seemed to promise success.

The plan was well laid. Two patriotic accomplices were found. One of them was to have a boat in readiness by the riverside. On the night fixed upon, they were to conceal themselves in Arnold's garden at midnight, seize and gag him when he came out for his nightly walk, and take him by way of the alley to the adjoining riverside. In case of meeting anyone and being questioned, it was arranged that they should profess to be carrying a drunken soldier to the guardhouse. Once in the boat, Hoboken could quickly be reached. Here, assistance from Lee's corps had been arranged.

The plot was a promising one. Champe prepared for it by removing some of the palings between the garden and the alley. These he replaced in such a way that they could be taken out again without noise. All being arranged, he wrote to Lee and told him that, on the third night from that date, if all went well, the traitor would be delivered upon the Jersey shore. He must be present, at an appointed place in the woods at Hoboken, to receive him.

This information gave Lee the greatest satisfaction. On the night in question, he left camp with a small party, taking with him four horses for the prisoner and his captors, and at midnight, sought the appointed spot. Here he waited with slowly declining hope. Hour after hour passed. The gray light of dawn appeared in the east, the sun rose over the waters, yet Champe and his prisoner failed to appear. Deeply disappointed, Lee led his party back to camp.

The cause of the failure may be told in a few words. It was a simple one. The very day which Champe had fixed for the execution of his plot, Arnold changed his quarters, his purpose being to attend to the embarkation of an expedition to the south, which was to be under his command.

In a few days, Lee received a letter from his agent telling the cause of failure and saying that, at present, success was hopeless. In fact, Champe found himself unexpectedly in an awkward situation.

Arnold's American legion was to form part of this expedition. Champe had enlisted in it. He was caught in a trap of his own setting. Instead of crossing the Hudson that night with Arnold as his prisoner, he found himself on board a British transport with Arnold as his commander. He was in the war on the British side, forced to face his fellow countrymen in the field.

We need not tell the story of Arnold's expedition to Virginia, with the brutal incidents which history relates concerning it. It will suffice to say that Champe formed part of it, all his efforts to desert proving fruitless. It may safely be said that no bullet from his musket reached the American ranks, but he was forced to brave death from the hands of those with whom alone he was in sympathy.

Not until Arnold's corps had joined Cornwallis at Petersburg did its unwilling recruit succeed in escaping. Taking to the mountains, he made his way into North Carolina, and was not long in finding himself among friends. His old corps was in that state, taking part in the pursuit of Lord Rawdon. It had just passed the Congaree in this pursuit when, greatly to the surprise of his old comrades, the deserter appeared in their ranks. Their surprise was redoubled when they saw Major Lee receive him with the utmost cordiality. A few minutes sufficed to change their surprise to admiration. There was no longer occasion for secrecy. Champe's story was told and was received with the utmost enthusiasm by his old comrades. So this was the man they had pursued so closely, this man who had been seeking to put the traitor within their hands. John Champe, they declared, was a comrade to be proud of, and his promotion to a higher rank was the plain duty of the military authorities.

Washington knew too well, however, what would be the fate of his late agent if taken by the enemy, to subject him to this peril. He would have been immediately hanged. Champe was, therefore, discharged from the service, after having been richly rewarded by the commander in chief. When Washington, seventeen years afterward, was preparing against a threatened war with the French, he sent to Lee for information about Champe, whom he desired to make a captain of infantry. He was too late. The gallant sergeant-major had joined a higher corps. He had enlisted in the grand army of the dead.

"God has given man wit to contrive, power to execute, and freedom of will to direct his conduct. It cannot be but that some, from a depravity of will, will abuse these privileges and exert these powers to the injury of others; and the oppressed would have no safety nor redress but by exerting the same powers in their defense, and it is our duty to set a proper value upon, and defend to the utmost, our just rights and the blessings of life. . . . for the most part, it (war) is undertaken to gratify the ambition of a prince, who wishes to subject to his arbitrary will a people whom God created free, and to gain an uncontrolled dominion over their rights and property."
~ Francis Hopkinson, A Political Catechism, *1777*

"The only means of establishing and perpetuating our republican forms of government is the universal education of our youth in the principles of Christianity by means of the Bible."
~ Benjamin Rush

"Far from being rivals or enemies, religion and law are twin sisters, friends, and mutual assistants. Indeed, these two sciences run into each other. The divine law, as discovered by reason and the moral sense, forms an essential part of both."
~ James Wilson

America the Beautiful

The words to this song were written by Katharine Lee Bates and the melody was written by Samuel Augustus Ward. Sing this song today.

Summer Countdown   Amy Puetz

July 1

The Rescue of a Redcoat

By Grace E. Craig, 1908

harity May a young Quaker girl stepped briskly to and fro before the spinning wheel which she had brought out to the front walk of the gray farmhouse on the hill. Occasionally, she lifted her brown eyes from her work and gazed out over the rolling pastures of the fair island of Prudence or across the strip of bay to the Rhode Island shore.

"It is a fine day, Polly," she said at length to the small girl who sat beside her sewing. "I think perhaps Mother will let us go out in the boat when our work is finished."

"Oh, Charity! Do you think she will?" asked little Polly and in her excitement, taking rather longer stitches than usual. "'Twill be beautiful on the bay this morning."

Charity studied the sea and sky intently.

"There's very little breeze stirring," she replied. "I am almost sure Mother will say we may go for a while if we do our work particularly well. Take care of those stitches, Poll. The last ones had best come out. They will never earn you an outing, but more like an extra long psalm."

Polly pouted, but in a moment laughed and pulled out the offending stitches, singing softly to herself as she set them again with great care. Charity worked with a will, and her task was soon finished. She disappeared into the house and, in a few moments, her voice rang merrily through the open door. "Mother says 'yes,' Polly. Put up your work for today."

Sweet Mother May followed her eldest daughter to the door and gazed lovingly after the two young figures. Though Charity was Polly's senior by five years, the sisters were loving comrades. They were both very happy when their brother Ben built them a boat. It was a rough craft but very seaworthy. Charity had strong young arms and soon became an expert with the oars, and even eight-year-old Polly quickly learned to pull away gallantly.

This morning the boat lay on the sand where Ben had left it after a fishing trip the day before. Polly, with a joyful giggle, climbed in and took her seat in the stern. Charity pushed off with little difficulty, and they were soon floating on Narragansett Bay. On this August morning, the warm, blue haze made all distant points vague and indistinct. Presently, Charity dropped her oars and sat still with clasped hands, and even Polly for once was quiet as the little boat drifted with the ebbing tide down toward Newport and the ocean.

"The French ships sailed out yesterday to meet Admiral Howe's squadron at sea, so Father was telling Ben last night," Charity said at last, breaking the long silence. "How can men fight and kill each other in this lovely summer weather?"

"Oh, Charity! Do they really do such dreadful things? Do you think it can be really true?" and Polly lifted a horrified face from the water, in which she had been dabbling her dimpled fingers, liberally sprinkling her gray gown and white kerchief.

"I fear it is, Polly," her sister answered with a shadow for a moment in her dark eyes. "Ben said he heard firing over in Portsmouth when he was out fishing yesterday."

A puff of wind coming over the water made Charity look up suddenly at the sun. "'Tis past noonday, Sis." she said. "We are a long way from home. We must start at once or Mother will worry."

Hastily picking up her oars, she turned the boat away from the nearby Portsmouth shore and headed for Prudence Island. As she settled herself for the long pull homeward, something on a point of land directly in front of her caught her eye. She held her oars suspended and looked again.

"That must be a signal of distress yonder," she finally said to her sister. "Turn about, Poll, and see what you can make of it."

Polly screwed her body around and gazed with wide, blue eyes. "I see naught, but a rag tied to a stick," she said. "How you frightened me, Charity!"

"Yes, but why should a rag be tied to a stick on that lonely point? Some poor creature must be in trouble. We will go and see."

"But, Charity," objected the little girl, "'Tis lonely there, as you say. And 'tis growing late, and the wind is rising. The bay is all white ruffles now. If we don't get home soon, I shall be afraid."

"Don't fear, little one," Charity soothed, "I will take care of you. Sit still now. We will be only a few moments and then, if we both row, I think we can get home before three." And she turned the boat again toward Portsmouth. Once on shore, she hesitated. Was she taking her little sister into peril?

"Would you rather sit in the boat and wait?" she asked.

"No, no," and Polly scrambled hastily out and caught her hand. "I'll not be left. I will go with you. We will take care of each other."

The two girls climbed the slope to the summit of a knoll, and there, a few feet away, was the little staff with its pitiful banner. They threaded their way through the tangle of bushes, stopping now and then to look and listen. All about the bayberry and sweet fern had been crushed and trampled as by heavy feet, but nothing broke the stillness of the summer noontide save the bees buzzing over the flowers and the crickets chirping in the grass.

"There must have been a skirmish here yesterday," Charity said.

Suddenly she stumbled and almost fell over something, and stopped with an exclamation. There, in the shelter of a thicket of bayberry, lay a man in the uniform of a British officer. Polly clung to her sister and began to cry loudly. At the sound of her weeping the man moved slightly and opened his eyes.

"Hush, little one," Charity whispered. "He cannot harm you. He is badly injured. His leg is broken, I think."

At her sister's assurance, Polly took courage and stopped crying. Coming closer, she examined admiringly the scarlet coat with its trimmings of gold. To the little Quaker lass, who had never before seen anything but plain garments, it seemed wonderful. But it was Charity's turn to look distressed.

"We must get him into the boat and take him home at once," she said.

"But how, Charity? He looks heavy," and Polly surveyed the prostrate man doubtfully.

"I don't know," answered her sister, "but we must find a way," and she gently touched the gold-braided sleeve. Again the soldier opened his eyes. Suddenly he made a weak effort to rise.

"Can you move a little, if we help you?" Charity asked, looking anxiously across the wide strip of water to Prudence Island. A fresh westerly wind had sprung up, and Polly's white ruffles of an hour ago had become whole caps now. Once more the soldier endeavored to rise, and this time, with the girls' help, succeeded.

Signers of the Declaration

Benjamin Franklin

1706–1790
Occupation – Printer and Scientist
Wife – Deborah Read
Children – 3
State – Pennsylvania

Benjamin Franklin was born in Boston but moved to Philadelphia in 1723. He only had enough money for three loaves of bread, and he walked through the streets with a loaf under each arm while he ate the third. He was a scientist and created the Franklin Stove. His experiments with electricity won him fame throughout the world. He used the penname Silence Dogood to write for his brother's paper. He created the *Poor Richard's Almanac*, which was popular in the American colonies. After signing the Declaration, he said, "We must all hang together, or most assuredly we shall all hang separately." He was sent to England to represent the colonies and he diligently worked to get the Stamp Act repealed. He served as an ambassador to France and helped form an alliance with that country. He negotiated the Treaty of Paris in 1783, which officially ended the War for Independence. He signed the Constitution. He once said, "Only a virtuous people are capable of freedom. As nations become corrupt and vicious, they have more need of masters." He had an illegitimate son who remained loyal to the crown, much to the disappointment of his father.

Signers of the Declaration

William Hooper

1742–1790
Occupation – Lawyer
Wife – Anne Clark
Children – 3
State – North Carolina

William Hooper was born in Boston and educated to become a minister but he chose to become a lawyer instead. He grew up in Boston and studied under James Otis, a patriotic man who helped pave the way for Independence. Hooper owned an estate called Finian. His house in Wilmington and his estate, Finian, were ransacked by the British. He lived the life of a fugitive while the British looked for him. His family also had to move from place to place to keep from being captured. He helped promote the ratification of the Constitution in 1788.

James Smith

1719–1806
Occupation – Lawyer
Wife – Eleanor Armor
Children – 5
State – Pennsylvania

James Smith learned surveying before becoming a lawyer. He pursued both careers. He helped raise a company of militia from his home state.

"If you can only get down to our boat," Charity urged, "we can take you home, and Mother will care for you."

"Come, poor soldier," Polly echoed. "Dear Mother will make you well."

A smile crossed the officer's pain-drawn face.

"Bless your dear heart, pretty one," he said.

Limping painfully with the stiffened leg dragging, he made his way to the beach, Charity just behind him, supporting him when he stopped to rest, and Polly by his side patting his red sleeve when she felt he needed encouragement. The man's breath came in gasps, but he smiled at his rescuers.

"Good little Samaritans," he whispered.

Suddenly Polly cried out, "Oh, Charity! Look, there's a storm coming!"

Sure enough. Over the high shoulder of Prudence Island, great masses of purple clouds were rolling heavily eastward. The wind was increasing almost to a gale too. A sudden, violent storm of the region was approaching.

"We must get home before it breaks." Charity spoke calmly, but for a moment her heartbeats quickened. "There is no shelter hereabouts."

Making a last, supreme effort the soldier rolled into the boat and fainted.

"Never mind him, Polly," Charity commanded. "You must take the other pair of oars and pull for dear life." A low growl of thunder in the west served to turn Polly's attention from their wounded passenger. She caught up her oars and rowed like the brave little woman she was.

"What time do you think it is, Charity?" she inquired once.

"After three a good bit," her sister answered.

"Mother will be worrying," the little girl said, with a slight shiver.

"Yes, Mother will be worrying," her sister repeated, looking over her shoulder at the approaching clouds. She fully realized what Polly only felt, that they were in a dangerous position.

Wind and tide were both against them, but they made good progress for some little time. The young man at their feet moaned now and then and moved uneasily, but the two rowers pulled steadily on.

"Mother will care for him once we reach home," Charity said, looking back again at the clouds, which had now rolled over the sun.

It grew suddenly dark on the bay, the wind died away slowly, and the sea became oily. In the lull, the rowers paused to rest. Suddenly a vivid flash of lightning rent the darkened sky, followed by a crashing peal of thunder. The girls in the boat sat motionless, petrified with terror. For a blinding, deafening moment, sea and sky seemed to meet. Then the squall shrieked down upon them in all its fury.

Charity's cap blew off, and her dark hair waved wildly about her face, but she flung the whole weight of her slender body upon the oars, pulling valiantly and shouting through the din for Polly to do the same. One moment of hesitation on the part of either would have been disastrous, but, guided by the two pairs of oars, the little craft kept afloat and rode out the gale. The worst of the wind was over in a few minutes, and then sheets of rain began to fall. Through the storm, the young mariners rowed bravely on toward the home shore and after half an hour of hard work, pulled into the calm water inside the point.

When the storm clouds had all rolled away, a rainbow spanned the bay as if promising a brighter future. The next day Charity and Polly, once more in spotless caps and kerchiefs, were sitting on the front step hand in hand.

"I'm glad we saved the young man," Polly remarked happily, "and I think his redcoat is very pretty, even though 'tis wicked."

"Dear little Poll," Charity answered with a half smile. "'Tis not wicked for him to wear a redcoat. He wears red, the color of his king, just as we wear the gray of the Friends."

"I wish Friends wore red then if 'tis not wicked. I like it," Polly said decisively.

"For shame, Polly," her sister admonished. "If Elder White should hear you, he would say again that mother is not strict enough with us."

Upstairs the British officer, his injury having been found to be only a bad strain, lay in Mother May's lavender-scented spare room. He was now fairly comfortable and had told his story.

When the French ships had been lured from Newport Harbor by the appearance of Admiral Howe's fleet, the British troops had marched out of the city and succeeded in driving the Americans from the island, though not without severe loss. In the battle on the downs, he, Sir Hugh Grantham, major in His Majesty's Sixty-third Foot Regiment, met with an accident. His horse was shot and fell instantly, pinning him beneath its body and injuring his right leg. He with difficulty crawled away from the scene of the combat, and, when the British retreated to the city, he was left unnoticed in his place of refuge under the

Benjamin Rush

1745–1813
Occupation – Physician
Wife – Julia Stockton
Children – 13
State – Pennsylvania

Benjamin Rush was called the "Father of American Medicine." He taught more than 2,000 pupils about medical treatment. One of his students was Meriwether Lewis. He served as the physician general of military hospitals in the Continental Army. He married the daughter of fellow signer Richard Stockton. He helped found the Philadelphia Bible Society. He helped found the Pennsylvania Society for Promoting the Abolition of Slavery in 1787. He aided in getting the Constitution ratified in his state. He said, "The great enemy of the salvation of man, in my opinion, never invented a more effective means of limiting Christianity from the world than by persuading mankind that it was improper to read the Bible at schools." Another time he said, "The Bible contains more knowledge necessary to man in his present state than any other book in the world."

bushes. Next day, he succeeded in dragging himself nearer the shore and hoisting a signal of distress, a bit of his shirt-sleeve tied to a stick.

The young soldier improved steadily under the kind care of the Quakers, and soon was able to limp downstairs, and often joined the children in their favorite place to work, just outside the front door. He proved a merry companion, telling many stories of his home across the sea—the old red manor house among the great oak trees, where his mother lived with his little sister Marjory, whom he declared Charity strongly resembled. Polly rejoiced greatly when he once more donned the beautiful red and gold coat.

"It is so bright," she said, patting it often. "I do like it."

"My little friend!" the British officer cried one day, "I believe you are a little turncoat. I think you would really change your peaceful gray for warlike red. Is it not so?"

"Yes," Polly admitted, "I would. Do you think I could be as good a girl in a red coat as in a gray one?"

"Perhaps," he answered gravely, "but certainly you could not be a braver little maid."

At last the day came for Father May to take Major Grantham over to Newport, whence he was to sail for England with his regiment, and two very sorrowful little lasses in white caps and kerchiefs watched their father's boat out of sight.

They missed their friend sadly, and they had not forgotten him when, in the early spring, a boat came up from Newport bringing letters and a large box which had just arrived from across the sea. The letters were from the major and his mother, thanking the Mays once more for their kindness to the wounded redcoat, praising the bravery of the little girls, and begging that the family accept the contents of the box with the heartfelt gratitude of the Granthams. Marjory sent many loving messages to Charity.

When the great box was opened, wonderful treasures were disclosed. Beautiful things such as the simple New England Friends had seldom seen. Books for Father May and the boys, fine linen and delicate china for the mother, some heavy silver spoons for Charity's hope chest, "just like Marjory's" the letters said, and down in the very bottom, something red. As Mother May drew it out, Polly began to dance.

"For me!" she cried, "is it not, Mother dear?"

Her mother looked at the label a little doubtfully, and then suddenly smiled as she saw her little girl's shining face. In another moment Polly was shaking out before the admiring eyes of the family a beautiful, long, scarlet cloak.

"May I wear it, Mother?" she begged.

And Mother May, wise woman that she was, still smiling, answered gently, "You may wear it sometimes, my dear."

And Polly did wear it until the Friends in Providence City heard of the frivolous red cloak down on Prudence Island and sent a stern letter of remonstrance to Mother May. Then it was laid carefully away and has been kept safely through many years, and Polly's great-great-grandchildren treasure it still as a memento of their little Revolutionary ancestor.

"The only foundation for a useful education in a republic is to be laid in religion. Without this there can be no virtue, and without virtue there can be no liberty, and liberty is the object and life of all republican governments." ~Benjamin Rush

"Christianity is the only true and perfect religion." ~Benjamin Rush

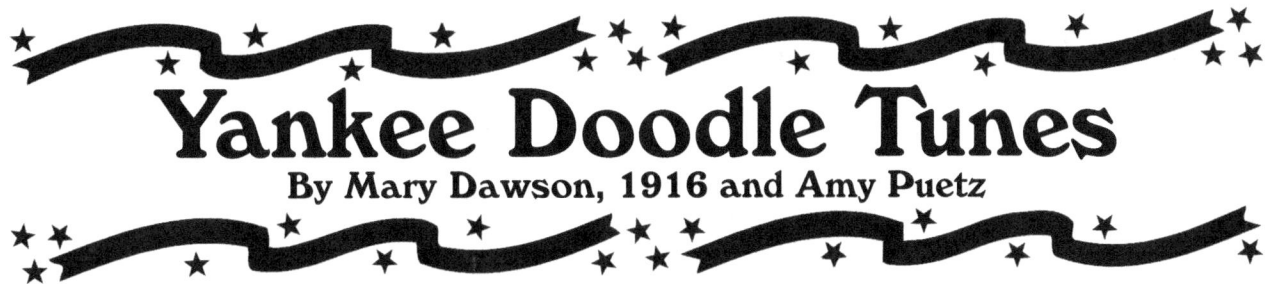

Yankee Doodle Tunes
By Mary Dawson, 1916 and Amy Puetz

A splendid contest in which both old and young can join together is one in which each player has a card with the name of some American song written on it and pinned on the back of his shirt. The tunes should be either patriotic or distinctively American, and each player's aim becomes to guess what tune is pinned to his back. This he can only do by listening attentively to what is whistled or hummed as he approaches or passes other players, for all are supposed to furnish such clues to assist fellow players in establishing their musical identity. The first player to communicate the correct name of the tune they wear to the person in charge of the game is the winner.

Some ideas of the tunes that may be used: "Yankee Doodle," "Star Spangled Banner," "God Bless America," "My Country 'Tis of Thee," "America the Beautiful," "This Land is Your Land," etc. Below are the songs on cards that may be copied.

- Yankee Doodle
- The Star Spangled Banner
- God Bless America
- My Country 'Tis of Thee
- America the Beautiful
- This Land is Your Land

July 2

An Escape from a Prison Ship

By Everett Titsworth Tomlinson, 1897

Thomas Andros was a prisoner on board the *Jersey*. In the summer of 1781 he had left his home in Massachusetts and, with some of the men in the congregation to which he preached, had joined the crew of a privateer. But only a few weeks had passed before the swift sloop was taken, and now the young preacher was a prisoner. His name was registered as soon as he reached the prison ship. He had been assigned to his place to eat with six others and then sent below into the hold.

As soon as his eyes became accustomed to the darkness, he looked about him at his fellow-prisoners, of whom there were a thousand at the time. Filth was on every side of him, and the air was so foul that he could hardly breathe. Many of his companions were ill, and dysentery, smallpox, and prison fever abounded. Vermin crawled over the filthy and tattered clothing of the men, and despair and hunger were expressed on almost every face.

"Hell can't be worse than this," said the young preacher, with a shudder, to the man nearest him.

"You may well say that," said the man, whom Andros perceived to be gray-headed. His face was thin, and his scanty clothing but partially covered his wasted form.

"Hell" was the name by which the *Jersey* came to be known, but neither knew it at the time.

"Is there no hope?" asked Andros.

"None," replied the man. "The British don't consider the crews of privateers as prisoners of war, and the Americans don't want to exchange able-bodied soldiers for such wrecks of men as you see here."

"But don't any escape?" said Andros.

"Not many from the *Jersey*. A few got away from the *Whitby* and *Good Hope*, but that has made the British more watchful. Nine sea captains and two privates on the *Good Hope* made a rush one night and disarmed the guard and made off in a yawl. They were fired upon but escaped in the darkness. Fifteen got away on the ice last winter, and others tried it but they couldn't stand the cold and were caught. One poor fellow was frozen to death before they could bring him back to the prison. A few others have gone, but not many."

All night long Andros could not sleep. It seemed to him that he was in torment, and the hopelessness of his companion's words was uppermost in his mind. He knew the *Jersey* was guarded by a captain, two mates, a cook, and a crew of a dozen sailors, and that in addition there were twelve old marines and thirty soldiers on board.

At daybreak the hatches were opened, and he heard the call, "Rebels, turn out your dead!"

The dead were selected from the living, each corpse was sewed in a blanket and carried to the shore under a guard and buried in a shallow grave. Andros, being one of the latest prisoners and presumably stronger, was selected as one of the men to assist in this sad duty. He returned to the ship with his heart bitter and resolved to escape or perish. To remain there was impossible!

In groups of six the men received their food. Moldy and wormy biscuit, damaged peas, some condemned beef or pork, with possibly a little sour meal, were measured out to each man and cooked in a huge copper kettle. Those who had a little money were able to purchase something in addition from an old woman who came on board each day.

But Thomas Andros, with all his sufferings, did not lose heart. No one knew what he had in mind, but he was ever on the watch. He was faithful and obedient, and none were suspicious of him. Two or three times he thought his opportunity had come, but he was prevented on each occasion.

One night, just at dusk, he was sent ashore with a guard for water. They landed on the shore of Long Island. Several times Andros carried his bucket full of water from the spring to the barrels in the yawl. As he started on his fourth trip, the guard became careless. Andros glanced all about him, and suddenly decided that his time had come. With a spring, he pushed the unsuspecting guard to the ground, and bounded swiftly toward the woods in the distance.

Signers of the Declaration

Arthur Middleton

1742–1787
Occupation – Planter
Wife – Mary Izard
Children – 9
State – South Carolina

Arthur Middleton was born at Middleton Place. Before the war, he traveled extensively in Europe. His family owned a large plantation, and this allowed him to travel to Rome, France, Spain, and other parts of Europe. The British plundered his plantation and destroyed his art collection. In 1779 Arthur Middleton was captured by the British and imprisoned at St. Augustine until 1781.

Francis Lightfoot Lee

1734–1797
Occupation – Planter
Wife – Rebecca Taylor
Children – none
State – Virginia

Francis Lightfoot Lee served in the House of Burgesses of Virginia. He also signed the Articles of Confederation. His estate, Menokin, was a wedding gift from his father-in-law. He was the younger brother of Richard Henry Lee.

In a moment, the guard regained his feet and fired at the fleeing preacher. Andros heard the bullet as it whistled past his head, but he did not falter. A shout brought the companions of the guard about him and the pursuit was begun. The prisoner knew he was too weak to run far or fast, and soon crept under a clump of bushes. On swept the pursuers. Would they discover him?

One almost stepped upon his crouching body, but the darkness favored him, and he was still unseen. He waited until they had gone, and then, quickly rising, ran with all his strength away from his place of concealment. Stumbling and falling in his weakness, he yet kept on until he heard the sound of approaching footsteps. He looked about for bushes, but none were to be seen. His only chance was to hide behind a tree and taking his stand there, he waited for the newcomer. If there were more than one, he knew he would be discovered. How his heart was beating! Surely it would be heard if his pursuers came near. There, he could see the man now, and he was coming directly toward the tree! But there was only one. Should he step forth and meet him?

He quickly decided that, as the man was armed and could summon aid, such a course would be useless, and his weakness would avail little against these men. No! His only course lay in concealment, and he waited for the man to approach. Nearer and nearer he came, and Andros slowly circled the tree. The guard drew near enough for him to have touched his arm, but he did not know how close the prisoner was and passed on.

For half an hour Andros waited, not daring to move. The only sounds he heard were the calls of the night birds and the whisperings of the wind. But he must not remain there and summoning all his strength, he again started on. But suppose he should lose his way? He did not know anything of the region except that it abounded in Tories, but on he must go. In a brief time he came to a highway and choosing, as he thought, the direction that led eastward he began to run.

What was that? A horseman was approaching. Had they aroused the neighborhood? He must take no chances, and he threw himself on the ground and tried to conceal himself in the high grass. The horseman was near now and was whistling as he came.

Suddenly the horse snorted and jumped aside. The rider, taken by surprise was thrown from his back. With an oath he leaped to his feet and caught the horse, which had not run far.

"What frightened you, Gypsy?" said the man. "You started as though you had seen a Whig. Don't you know the difference between a man and a log yet? But I'll see what it was," and he began to search along the roadside.

"Surely," thought Andros, "now I shall be found," but in a few minutes the man abandoned his search and, quickly remounting, rode away.

Again Andros arose and pushed forward in the darkness. He must not delay now. All night the wretched prisoner kept on, now running, and now compelled to stop from exhaustion. The next day he rested until afternoon, but he was almost famished. Food he must have, and at last he approached a house by the roadside. His knock was answered, and he entered. A man, evidently a tailor, was working at a table and near him was his wife.

"I am almost starving, my good woman. Will you feed me?"

A bowl of bread and milk was placed before him and the preacher ate as only a famished man can. He did not look up until the bowl was empty, and then he discovered that the man was gone.

"Here, take this," said the woman, placing an apple pie in his hands. "I don't want to know who you are. Don't tell me, but don't stay here."

His strength somewhat restored now, Andros needed no second bidding and ran up the road. He soon came to a clump of trees and resolved to hide and wait for a time there. And it was well that he did, for in a few moments two men on horseback approached and halted near enough for him to hear their words. His heart sank as he recognized the tailor as one of the men.

"I'm sure he was an escaping prisoner," said the tailor, "and he started up this way."

"We'll soon overtake him then," replied his companion, and they started up the road.

"I'll wait until they come back," thought Andros, but as they did not come when the darkness fell, he resumed his flight. His apple pie served until the next day and then he knew he must try again. He approached a respectable-looking house and a woman met him at the door. She listened to his request for food and then said, "Get out, or I'll set the dog on you. Maybe you're the man that escaped from the *Jersey* I've heard about. Here, Maje!" she called to the dog.

Andros turned and ran, with the dog swiftly pursuing. He stopped when he found he could run no farther and,

James Wilson

1742–1798
Occupation – Lawyer
Wives – Rachel Bird and Hannah Gray
Children – 7
State – Pennsylvania

James Wilson taught Latin at the College of Philadelphia. He also signed the Constitution and ardently worked to get it ratified in his state. He helped recruit soldiers to fight in the Continental army. He once said, "Man does not exist for the sake of government, but government is instituted for the sake of man." Another time he said, "Human law must rest its authority ultimately upon the authority of that law which is Divine."

Thomas Lynch Jr.

1749–1779
Occupation – Lawyer
Wife – Elizabeth Shubrich
Children – none
State – South Carolina

Thomas Lynch Jr. had a plantation called Peach Tree Plantation. His father was a delegate to the Continental Congress but when he had a stroke Thomas was asked to fill his shoes. Thomas contracted a fever while trying to recruit soldiers for the Revolution. He died when only thirty years old while sailing with his wife to France for his health.

Signers of the Declaration

Robert Morris

1734–1806
Occupation – Merchant
Wife – Mary White
Children – 7
State – Pennsylvania

Robert Morris was against independence and didn't show up the day of the vote so his voice wouldn't put Pennsylvania as a no. Afterward he joined wholeheartedly into the cause of freedom. He did more than any other man to keep the young United States going. He worked with the states to give money and supplies, he borrowed money from friends with a personal guarantee that they would get the money back, he gave his personal fortune to cover expenses. He was called the "Financier of the Revolution," even though he died penniless. As a merchant, he and his firm were contracted by the Continental Congress to import arms and ammunition in 1775. He also signed the Articles of Confederation and the Constitution. Although offered the job of Secretary of the Treasury by George Washington, he served as a senator in the first congress under the Constitution in 1789.

with all his strength, flung a stone. The dog howled and, with drooping tail, turned and ran down the road.

On and on went Andros, spurred, now by the knowledge that his escape was known. For an hour he ran but could go no farther. "I'll try once more," he said, and approached a house in which he could see a light.

In response to his request, he was admitted, and a benevolent-looking old lady, without a word, placed food before him. A bowl of bread and milk, a dried bluefish roasted, and a mug of cider soon disappeared. Bedtime came. The old man took his Bible and read aloud and then all stood up while he prayed.

"I'll tell them," thought Andros, and then he told his story.

A flood of tears was the answer of the old lady and then she said, "Husband, let us burn his clothes."

The old man threw fresh wood on the fire, and his wife wrapped the prisoner in blankets and placed his filthy clothing in the huge oven. Soon the feeble man was asleep in a clean bed and resting like a tired babe.

The next day the old man gave Andros some of his clothes and helped Andros on his journey. When at last he arrived at Sag Harbor, he found friends who carried him across the Sound and, at last, he made his way to his home in Berkley.

"Oh Thomas! Where have you been?" said his wife, with a wild cry, as the tottering man stood before her.

"I've been in hell," answered Andros as he fell in a swoon.

For many long weeks they nursed him through the fever that followed, not knowing that the name he had given the *Jersey* had clung to her, and that among the colonies she never ceased to be so called.

Thomas Andros recovered, but, for years, the story of his escape was a thrilling tale in the new nation.

In his autobiography he wrote, "Some time in the latter part of October 1781, I arrived at home. And near the close of winter I so far regained my health, through the great kindness of the God of love, as to engage in the instruction of a school in the town where I resided; and since that period, almost my whole life has been devoted to the instruction of youth and preaching the everlasting Gospel. And whether my life has been in any degree useful, or whether it would have been, as to the glory of God and the good of mankind, as well that I should have made my grave in the *Old Jersey*, will doubtless be made manifest in the last day."

Signers Quiz

Match the signers on the left with the state they represented on the right. Answers are below.

1. Joseph Hewes, William Hooper, and John Penn
2. Thomas McKean, George Read, and Caesar Rodney
3. Samuel Huntington, Roger Sherman, William Williams, and Oliver Wolcott
4. Button Gwinnett, Lyman Hall, and George Walton
5. Carter Braxton, Benjamin Harrison, Thomas Jefferson, Francis Lightfoot Lee, Richard Henry Lee, Thomas Nelson Jr., and George Wythe
6. Charles Carroll, Samuel Chase, William Paca, and Thomas Stone
7. Abraham Clark, John Hart, Francis Hopkinson, Richard Stockton, and John Witherspoon
8. George Clymer, Benjamin Franklin, Robert Morris, John Morton, George Ross, Benjamin Rush, James Smith, George Taylor, and James Wilson
9. William Floyd, Francis Lewis, Philip Livingston, and Lewis Morris
10. William Ellery and Stephen Hopkins
11. Thomas Heyward Jr., Thomas Lynch Jr., Arthur Middleton, and Edward Rutledge
12. Samuel Adams, John Adams, Elbridge Gerry, John Hancock, and Robert Treat Paine
13. Josiah Bartlett, Matthew Thornton, and William Whipple

A. Georgia
B. New York
C. Connecticut
D. Pennsylvania
E. Massachusetts
F. Virginia
G. New Hampshire
H. Delaware
I. South Carolina
J. Maryland
K. New Jersey
L. North Carolina
M. Rhode Island

These five men formed the committee that created the Declaration of Independence: John Adams, Roger Sherman, Robert Livingston, Thomas Jefferson, and Benjamin Franklin

Answers
1-L. North Carolina
2-H. Delaware
3-C. Connecticut
4-A. Georgia
5-F. Virginia
6-J. Maryland
7-K. New Jersey
8-D. Pennsylvania
9-B. New York
10-M. Rhode Island
11-I. South Carolina
12-E. Massachusetts
13-G. New Hampshire

July 3

Tench Tilghman's Ride

By Jams Baldwin, 1916

It was mid-autumn in Virginia in the year 1781. In the low-lying peninsula of the York, the weather was still warm with not even a hint of frost to color the dying leaves in the woods and orchards. But there had been rain, and the old south road, formerly so firm and smooth, was little else than a succession of mud holes and deep wagon ruts winding through the pine woods, among bogs and over causeways, and losing itself in an ocean of mire. For of late there had been much travel in this direction—armed men on foot and on horseback, supply wagons, country folk with fodder and the courage of curiosity—all pressing forward to the aid of the patriots under General Washington who were besieging Lord Cornwallis and his redcoats behind the redoubts at Yorktown.

To the few people who remained at Williamsburg, eleven miles away, this was a time of anxiety and doubt. Day after day they heard the sullen roar of cannon sounding like muffled thunder in the distance and, night after night, they watched the reflection of the campfires dimly illuming the sky above the dark pine forest. On the steps of the old tavern and under the trees of the college green, a few old men and cripples and boys loitered and listened, now and then exchanging anxious guesses about what was going on at Yorktown. Some reckoned that the redcoats were sure to win, and others timidly expressed the hope that something would happen to aid the patriots and end this miserable war.

But one day—it was the nineteenth of October—there came a change. A threatening silence filled the air and rested on field and town, on earth and sky. There was no far away sound of booming cannon, the road through the pines was deserted, even the sounds of labor were hushed.

At Williamsburg and the nearby plantations, everybody stopped and wondered.

"Something's happened," whispered one.

"Yes, or something's going to happen," agreed another.

"What can it be?" asked a third.

And the little anxious groups at the tavern door and along the wayside, gazed southward and wondered what would come to pass next. Suddenly, just beyond the first turn in the road, a faint sound was heard disturbing the painful silence. Very indistinct it was, like the beating of a drum or the rapid splashing of an oar far away. But it was not a drum, it was not an oar. It came nearer, rapidly, then ceased, then was heard again much more distinctly.

"It's a horse galloping over the long crossway and then struggling through the mud," said the innkeeper. "Maybe it's the Americans on the retreat, with the redcoats following behind."

"Then we may as well be getting out of this place," said the old sexton, hobbling quickly away toward the church.

The next moment the horseman was in plain sight, emerging from behind a thicket of scrubby pines not forty rods away. Immediately he was at the lower end of the

George Wythe

1726–1806
Occupation – Lawyer
Wives – Ann Lewis
and Elizabeth Taliafero
Children – 1
State – Virginia

George Wythe taught many of the nation's leaders including Thomas Jefferson, James Monroe, John Marshall, and Henry Clay. He served in the Virginia House of Burgesses. He designed the Virginia seal which had a picture of a man standing over a king with the words, *Sic Semper Tyrannis* which is Latin for "thus always to tyrants." He freed his adult slaves, and in his will, he freed the children. His will also provided for the freed blacks. He died strangely and suddenly in 1806. Many believed that his grandnephew and heir poisoned him. He attended the Constitutional Convention but did not sign it although he helped see to it that it was ratified by Virginia once it was signed.

street, riding easily but swiftly. In his hand he waved a small flag, the emblem of America, and as he drew rein near the tavern door, he shouted, "Good news, good news, my friends! Cornwallis is taken at Yorktown. Cornwallis has surrendered with his whole army."

"Hooray!" shouted the innkeeper. "We're mighty glad to see you, Colonel Tilghman. Won't you alight and tell us all about it?"

The horseman dismounted for a few moments, just to tighten the saddle girths and give his horse a sip of water and a breathing spell.

"Hooray! Hooray!" shouted everybody, and the timid ones, even women and children, came running to hear the good news. "Cornwallis is taken. Hooray for General Washington! Hooray!"

"I reckon it's a big victory for our side," remarked the sexton, coming bravely up and breathing hard. "Hadn't I better ring the bell?"

"Yes, it's the greatest victory of the war," said the horseman, remounting. "Seven thousand, the main part of the British army, with all their arms and supplies! It's a big victory, a decisive victory. It means independence for us."

"Hooray! Hooray!" shouted everyone.

"And I suppose you're just riding around to tell folks about it, ain't you?" exclaimed one of the most inquisitive.

"I'm riding to Philadelphia to carry General Washington's message to the Continental Congress there," replied the horseman. Then a word to his steed, and he was away, galloping toward Fredericksburg.

"I know that man," said the innkeeper. "It's Colonel Tench Tilghman of Maryland. He is Washington's right-hand man, and they do say that the general trusts him more than he does anyone else. He's the right man to carry the news to Congress. He kept store up there at Philadelphia before the war, and he knows everybody."

"It's a long way to Philadelphia, ain't it?" asked the inquisitive man.

"More than two hundred and fifty miles," answered the innkeeper. "It's a mighty long way, a mighty long way."

"And bad roads too," added the sexton. "It takes more than a week to go there, even in dry weather."

"But Tench Tilghman, he'll ride it much quicker. He's a good horseman, and he knows the way."

"Hooray! Hooray for Washington and Tench Tilghman. Boys, let's hoist the new flag! Independence forever!"

And Colonel Tilghman, with his face set northward, rode steadily on. The roads in those days were not as we know them now. They were little more than pathways or wagon tracks winding through the woods and between the straggling plantations, and there were hills to climb and rivers to ford. More than once the rider was obliged to stop and inquire the way. But everywhere the news of his coming seemed to fly before him. Men and boys were waiting at the crossroads or sitting on the fences by the

Richard Henry Lee

1732–1794
Occupation – Planter
Wives – Anne Aylet and
Anne Gaskins Pinckard
Children – 9
State – Virginia

Richard Henry Lee made the motion that "these united colonies are and of right ought to be free and independent states." He also signed the Articles of Confederation and was a Senator from Virginia. He once said, "It is certainly true that a popular government cannot flourish without virtue in the people." He raised a group of militia during the French and Indian War and offered to join General Braddock. Instead of accepting the Virginians' help, Braddock refused to allow them to march with him. Lee influenced Congress to appoint George Washington as the commander in chief of the army.

way, or loitering upon their doorsteps, and to all these he shouted as he rode past, "Good news! Cornwallis is taken."

All day long he rode, stopping only for a few moments now and then at some friendly farmhouse or roadside inn. Fifty miles, sixty miles, seventy miles, and his horse began to fail. He must have another. To the patriot planter to whom he applied for help, he had only to say, "Cornwallis is taken at Yorktown. I carry dispatches to the Continental Congress at Philadelphia." The fresh horse was provided and, with renewed vigor, he pushed forward, through the gathering gloom, to Fredericksburg.

It was late in the night, but the news spread through the town like wildfire. "Hooray! Cornwallis is taken at Yorktown. So says Colonel Tilghman, who is on his way to tell it to the Congress." A big gun was fired. Men and boys, with fife and drum, marched through the streets rejoicing. Bonfires were lighted. Nobody at Fredericksburg slept that night.

At daybreak the journey was resumed. The horse was fresh, the roads were good, and the brave messenger pushed forward with relentless courage. At Mount Vernon, he stopped long enough to deliver letters to the mistress of the house and to relate in detail the story of the surrender. And there, another change of horses took place and a strong and fresh steed from Washington's own stables was saddled and bridled for the long ride.

At Alexandria half the journey was accomplished. Here and at Arlington, later the home of the Lees, the news was repeated: "Victory is ours, for Cornwallis is taken at Yorktown."

Another night and then onward, across the Potomac where the capital of the nation would afterward arise in splendor. Onward, through Maryland to Baltimore and beyond, and everywhere the cry was repeated with varying notes of rejoicing: "Hooray! Hooray! Washington has won at Yorktown, and the war must end."

Signers of the Declaration

Edward Rutledge

1749–1800
Occupation – Lawyer and Planter
Wives – Henrietta Middleton and Mary Eveleigh
Children – 3
State – South Carolina

At first he was against breaking away from England. He wanted the colonies to have some foreign aid before taking the step of independence. But when he saw that the Declaration of Independence would be adopted, he made sure that South Carolina voted for it. He married Henrietta Middleton, the sister of fellow signer Arthur Middleton. He was the youngest signer. He served as the governor of South Carolina after the war.

It was on the nineteenth of October that the surrender was completed. It was past midnight of the twenty-third when Tench Tilghman, with Washington's dispatches in his saddlebags, rode weary but unfaltering into Philadelphia. All the good people were fast asleep. The streets were dark and, but for the light of the failing moon, they would have been impassable. There was no sound save the thud of the horse's iron-shod hoofs upon the unpaved roadway. But Tench Tilghman was no stranger there. He had lived for years in the old town and sold merchandise there, and every street and alley—yes, every house and dooryard—was familiar to him. He rode, somewhat slowly, down the street of chestnuts, not meeting a soul nor seeing even the glimmer of a tallow candle. He turned into Second Street and then into High, where stood the house of Thomas McKean, the president of the Continental Congress.

Right there, he met the town watch, in whose care the entire city was safely sleeping. With a tin lantern in one hand and a short hickory staff in the other, the officer was plodding along in the middle of the street, stopping at each corner to sing out the hour, "Past two o'clock, and all is well in the morning!"

The sight of a man on horseback startled him in the midst of his cry, "Past two o'clock," and stopping suddenly, he raised his staff to impress the rider with a due sense of the terrors of the law.

"Halt! Where are you going?" he demanded.

"To the house of Thomas McKean," answered Tench Tilghman, "and I see that I am already there."

He alighted from the saddle and threw the bridle reins over the hitching post in front of a large square house which loomed up, dark and quite alone, in the dim moonlight.

"Halt!" again demanded the watchman. "I am constrained to arrest you for disturbing the peace and quiet of the town at this unseemly hour. I must commit you to the jail until such time as the magistrate may be pleased to deal with you."

He again raised his staff, but Tench Tilghman gently pushed him aside and, going up to the door, made such a rapping with the big brass knocker as had not been heard in that street for many a day. But no sound came from the sleepers within.

"I warn you, friend—" began the watchman.

Tench Tilghman knocked again, louder, harder, more persistent than before. An upper window was raised, and a head wearing a nightcap was timidly protruded.

"Who's there? What's the matter?"

"I am Colonel Tilghman, and I bring important dispatches to the Continental Congress and President McKean. Cornwallis is taken at Yorktown, and victory is ours!"

The next moment the door was thrown wide open, and Thomas McKean himself, in his night attire, with a lighted candle in his hand, rushed out to greet the message bearer.

"What's that, Colonel Tilghman? What did you say?"

"Cornwallis is taken at Yorktown and victory is ours!" was the brief reply, and there was a hearty handshaking as the colonel was ushered inside, and the door closed behind him.

"Well, there, I ought to have known old Tench Tilghman but I didn't," muttered the watchman, as he picked up his lantern and resumed his walk.

"Past two o'clock in the morning; and Cornwallis is taken at Yorktown!" he shouted so loudly that the whole town rang with his cry and the people, hurriedly rising, ran out into the street to repeat the good news.

Neighbors joined with neighbors, and groups gathered at every street corner, talking and shouting and shivering in the frosty moonlight.

"Hooray! Hooray! Three cheers for General Washington and liberty! Cornwallis is taken at Yorktown."

Presently, someone suggested a procession. Drums and fifes and flags were brought out, and Chestnut Street was not wide enough to hold the multitude of marchers and onlookers that filled the early hours of that October morning with sounds of rejoicing. Then the old statehouse bell was set in motion, and its deep-toned clanging, together with the roar of cannon, roused the country folk, beyond the Schuylkill and beyond the Delaware, and set them to wondering what had happened in the quiet city at so early an hour.

"Past two o'clock," still shouted the old watchman, forgetful of the time, "and all is well in the morning! Cornwallis is taken at Yorktown, and independence is won!"

And what more shall be said of Colonel Tench Tilghman? The Continental Congress, convening early in the morning, listened with breathless interest to the dispatches of which he was the bearer and, later, the delegates voted to present him a fine new horse and an elegant sword, as tokens of their appreciation.

My Country 'Tis of Thee

This song was written in 1831 by Samuel Francis Smith. Sing this song today.

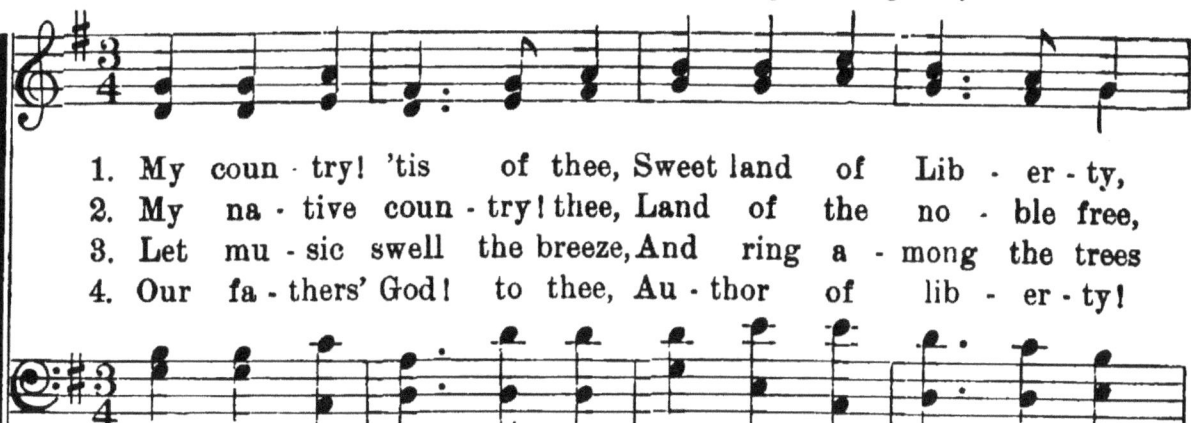

1. My country! 'tis of thee, Sweet land of Liberty,
2. My native country! thee, Land of the noble free,
3. Let music swell the breeze, And ring among the trees
4. Our fathers' God! to thee, Author of liberty!

Of thee I sing; Land where my fathers died; Land of the
Thy name I love; I love thy rocks and rills, Thy woods and
Sweet freedom's song: Let mortal tongues awake, Let all that
To thee we sing; Long may our land be bright With freedom's

pilgrim's pride; From ev-'ry mountain-side Let freedom ring.
templed hills, My heart with rapture thrills Like that above.
breathe partake, Let rocks their silence break, The sound prolong.
holy light, Protect us by thy might, Great God, our King!

Summer Countdown   Amy Puetz

July 4

The Rescue of Old Glory

By Mrs. J. W. Wheeler, 1918

When Mother was making plans for a "safe and sane Fourth."

Uncle Henry said, "Why not take the children to the park and have a kite party? I'll help them make the kites."

The next morning Harry and Anna were busy out on the porch with Uncle Henry. By ten o'clock three handsome white kites were drying in a row. Anna called them the "Big Bear, the Middle-Sized Bear, and the Baby Bear."

When the kites were dry, the whole family started for the park—Uncle Henry with the Big Bear and a box of luncheon, Harry with the Middle-Sized Bear, and Anna, of course, with the Baby Bear. Mother carried some sewing and Grandmother carried the surprise, something that Uncle Henry had brought home in a flat box. When they reached the park, they found a gathering of people. A tent was up, the band was playing, the older boys were shooting at a target, and the little boys and girls were flying red and blue balloons.

Uncle Henry said, "Ladies first, always," and he soon had the Baby Bear in the air, and the string in Anna's hands. He drove the bobbin into the ground, to make sure that the kite would not get away. Harry insisted upon putting his kite up alone. Then Uncle Henry put up the Big Bear, and when it was up some distance, he asked Grandmother to open the box. Then he shook out a red, white, and blue silk American flag, and the crowd cheered.

Uncle Henry tied the flag to a loop of string and fastened it to the Big Bear's string. Then he let it out, hand over hand. Up, up, went Old Glory and snapped in the breeze. The higher it went, the farther out the kite soared, until it hung over the harbor. They were all so busy watching it that they had not seen that the picnic people below were pointing up to the flag but when the band struck up the "Star Spangled Banner," and the people began to sing, Uncle Henry noticed one dark-skinned boy who sang with a strange accent and great energy, and who kept his big, solemn eyes on the flag that glowed against the sky. But when the boy, whose name was Caspar, saw the others looking at him, he ran down the hill and hid behind the children.

"Anyone who can sing the "Star Spangled Banner" like that is a good American," said Uncle Henry, as he drove his bobbin into the ground, and prepared to open the picnic.

When the other picnickers went in to dinner, Caspar did not follow. He took his sandwiches, frosted cake, and

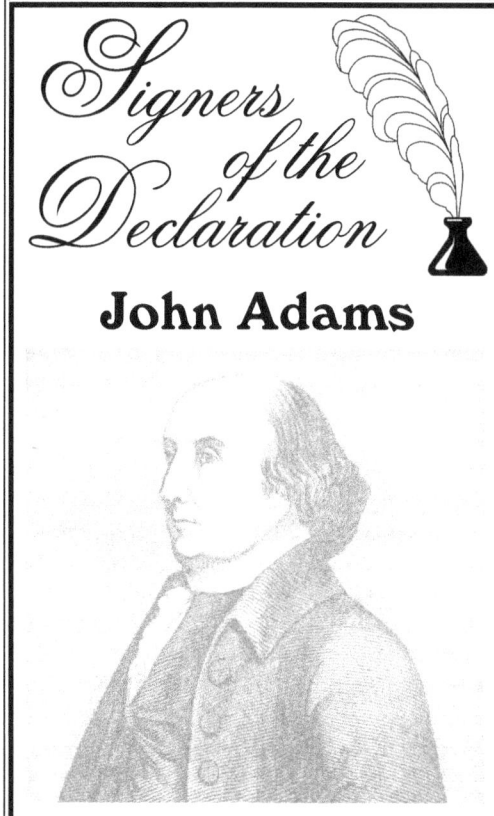

Signers of the Declaration

John Adams

1735–1826
Occupation – Lawyer
Wife – Abigail Smith
Children – 5
State – Massachusetts

John Adams was the U. S. Minister to France and England, the first vice–president, and the second president. He defended the British soldiers who were involved in the Boston Massacre. He, along with Benjamin Franklin and John Jay, negotiated the Treaty of Paris, which ended the American Revolution. He once said, "The general principles on which the Fathers achieved independence were the general principles of Christianity." He was the first president to live in the White House. When he moved into the new house, he said, "I pray Heaven to bestow the best of blessings on this house and all that shall hereafter inhabit it. May none but honest and wise men ever rule under this roof." He once said, "I have examined all religions, and the result is that the Bible is the best book in the world."

Signers of the Declaration

Thomas Jefferson

1743–1826
Occupation – Planter
Wife – Martha Skelton
Children – 6
State – Virginia

Thomas Jefferson had an estate called Monticello. He enjoyed playing the violin. He was the governor of Virginia, an ambassador to France, and the third president. He lost his wife during the war. Many believe her health declined from having to flee from the British. He once said, "Liberty to worship our Creator in the way we think most agreeable to His will (is) a liberty deemed in other countries incompatible with good government and yet proved by our experience to be its best support." During his presidency, he said, "No nation has ever yet existed or been governed without religion—nor can be. The Christian religion is the best religion that has been given to man, and I, as Chief Magistrate of this nation, am bound to give it the sanction of my example." He and John Adams died on the 50th anniversary of the signing of the Declaration in 1826.

ice cream, and sat down on the grass, where he could look at the flag.

There was not a child in the whole park who loved the Stars and Stripes as little Caspar did, not even the two American children; for in his own country Caspar had lived in a mission house, where they had told him all about America and how the Stars and Stripes protected the people, even the poorest of little children. They told him that he must never harm the flag or allow it to be trampled on. After he came to America, his teacher taught him to salute the flag.

He had heard the flag song on the big ship, and he felt that it was Old Glory that had brought him safe to one of his own countrywomen in America, with whom he lived.

Caspar was thinking of all this as he reclined on the grass and saw the flag fluttering in the light wind. He had watched it for some time, when he saw it give a quick little shiver, then begin to sink slowly, and then faster. He looked to the end of the line and saw that the great white kite was

Our cause is just. Our union is perfect. Our internal resources are great, and, if necessary, foreign assistance is undoubtedly attainable. We gratefully acknowledge, as signal instances of the Divine favor towards us, that His Providence would not permit us to be called into this severe controversy, until we were grown up to our present strength, had been previously exercised in warlike operation, and possessed of the means of defending ourselves. With hearts fortified with these animating reflections, we most solemnly, before God and the world, declare that, exerting the utmost energy of those powers which our beneficent Creator hath graciously bestowed upon us, the arms we have been compelled by our enemies to assume, we will, in defiance of every hazard, with unabating firmness and perseverance, employ for the preservation of our liberties; being with one mind resolved to die freemen rather than to live slaves.

With an humble confidence in the mercies of the supreme and impartial Judge and Ruler of the Universe, we most devoutly implore His divine goodness to protect us happily through this great conflict, to dispose our adversaries to reconciliation on reasonable terms, and thereby to relieve the empire from the calamities of civil war.

Declaration of the Causes and Necessity of Taking up Arms *by Thomas Jefferson July 6, 1775*

dipping about in a strange manner, then he looked up to the hill and saw the kite man leaping down the slope as fast as he could. The American children were running behind him.

Caspar trembled with excitement. What would happen to the flag? Would it get trampled upon, or would it go out to sea and get wet and spoiled? Oh, he must help them get Old Glory! He ran until he was directly beneath the flag; then he stretched his arms high to catch it if it fell. But a strong breeze came up and carried the Big Bear over the water, pulling the flag with it. Caspar ran on to the water's edge.

Caspar did not know what to do next. There were no people on the shore, and no boats were near. The flag had not been trampled on, but it might fall in the water any minute. Where were the people? Did they know that a great calamity was about to happen to everybody in the park, to everybody in America, perhaps to the mission ladies who had been so good to him? How could the people sit about, eating and drinking when there was such trouble in the world? He cried out to Uncle Henry and the children, who were now quite near, strange and broken words, and he tried to tell them that he could not swim.

"Good boy, swim for it! You'll get it!" shouted Uncle Henry.

Caspar understood the word swim but not the rest. He thought the kite man must be telling him that he could not swim either. He looked out to the flag; it was surely going into the water; it flapped and dipped, then dipped deeper still, right into the water. Caspar did not wait another minute. Off went his jacket, and with a wild look toward the shore, he ran into the water. His feet slipped on the sandy bottom, and the kite jerked up, then down, then up—but it was always just out of reach.

They watched the boy, who was trying hard to keep the flag in sight.

"Hurry, hurry, Uncle Henry, he can't swim a stroke!" shouted Harry.

Uncle Henry was just in time. Caspar had a firm hold on Old Glory and came up tangled in its folds.

After Uncle Henry had shaken the water out of the boy, he sat him on his shoulder where everybody could see him. "Now, one, two, three!" he said, as he waved his free arm. "All cheer for the boy who would not let the flag be lost even if he couldn't swim! Hooray!"

"Hooray! Hooray! Hooray!" they said and then they cheered all over again, and crowded around Uncle Henry and Caspar until the pair started home to put on dry clothes.

When little Caspar went home that night, he carried the flag that he had saved. Grandmother had washed and dried it, and it looked as good as new.

Signers of the Declaration

Thomas Heyward Jr.

1746–1809
Occupation – Lawyer
Wives – Elizabeth Matthews and Elizabeth Savage
Children – 8
State – South Carolina

Thomas Heyward Jr. had a plantation called White Hall Plantation. It was plundered by the British and all his slaves were taken. During the British attack on Port Royal Island in 1779, he was wounded. He was captured after the fall of Charleston and taken to St. Augustine. Just before his release in 1781, he wrote new verses for the British national anthem, "God Save the King." His version was "God save the thirteen States," and it was sung in all the colonies. He also signed the Articles of Confederation.

Racing for the Flag
By Mary Dawson, 1916 and Amy Puetz

For younger boys and girls, nothing could be better than some new and exciting race games grouped together and called Racing for the Flag. For these you will need about a dozen medium-sized cotton flags of the inexpensive kind, sold everywhere before the Fourth. One flag at a time is placed upright in the turf, and six youngsters contest in a race to obtain it.

Six boys may lead off with the first race, and six girls can follow with the second one. Each race is handicapped in some hilarious way, and elders, acting as spectators, will enjoy the feature almost as much as the youthful contestants. Here are some of the comic handicaps which might be arranged, alternating boys and girls.

Boys race with potato sacks drawn up over their knees and tied around the waist or under the arms. The course to be covered need not be long.

Girls race backward or blindfolded. None must turn around until her name is called. The course should be short.

Boys race in sacks; if the game is played on the soft turf they might race creeping on hands and knees.

Girls race hopping on the right foot.

Boys race hopping on the left foot.

Girls race as partners, each team holding opposite ends of a clothespin.

Boys race with feet hobbled with tricolored ribbon, allowing for very short steps.

Girls race winding balls of twine, which have been slacked out between the flags and the starting point. The competitors are not permitted to move faster than they can wind.

Where the lack of turf makes any of these sports difficult to arrange, you might substitute races on roller skates, in one of which, for instance, each has a partner who is holding onto opposite ends of a handkerchief.

Of course each boy or girl retains all the flags they capture, and a prize may be awarded for the greatest number of flags captured.

Index

Activities
American Revolution Quiz, 102
Famous Fathers Quiz, 63
Famous Mothers Quiz, 17
Father's Day Activities, 59
Heroes of the Civil War Quiz, 28
Making a Five-Pointed Star, 44
Memorial Day (decorate the grave of a soldier), 35
Remembering, 21
Signers Quiz, 131

Authors
Bailey, Carolyn Sherwin, 3, 16, 45, 70
Baldwin, James, 15, 94, 132
Blaisdell, Albert, 65, 78, 82, 103, 107
Blaisdell and Ball, 78
Colton, Arthur Willis, 22
Craig, Grace E., 119
Fassett, James Hiram, 56
Ford, Harry Pringle, 43
Hartwell, Clark, 62
Hurlbut, Jesse Lyman, 61
Jewett, Sarah Orne, 29
Johonnot, James, 77
Kingsley, Florence Morse, 8
La Bree, Ben, 19
Lay, Dorothea, 42
Lindsay, Maud, 51
Longfellow, Henry Wadsworth, 82
Lossing, Benson John, 98
Means, Celina Eliza, 92
Morris, Charles, 89, 111
Ogden, H. A., 37
Roosevelt, Theodore, 58
Tomlinson, Everett Titsworth, 126
Wheeler, Mrs. J. W., 138

Cooking
Fruity Flag, 87
Star Sandwiches, 110

Crafts
Cocked Hat, 106
Felt Flag Puzzle, 40
Ladies Cap, 93
Make a Father's Day Card, 54
Make a Mother's Day Card, 13
Making a Five-Pointed Star, 44
Star Craft, 80

Games
Find the Cards, 97
Games for Mother's Day, 7
Racing for the Flag Game, 142
The Tricolor Game, 69
Yankee Doodle Tunes Game, 125

Holidays
Father's Day, 50-63
Flag Day, 36-48
Fourth of July, 64-141
Independence Day, 64-142
Memorial Day, 18-35
Mother's Day, 2-17

Motto of the American Revolution, 86

Poems
"Daddies" by Edgar A. Guest, 53
"The Dead Volunteer" by J. W. Barker, 28
"The Fallen" by John Vance Cheney, 27
"The Man to Be" by Edgar A. Guest, 62
"Memorial Day" by Jane Campbell, 35
"The Real Successes" by Edgar A. Guest, 57
"A Song for Our Flag" by Margaret E. Sangster, 42

Quotes
Adams, Abigail, 93
Adams, John, 96
Bartlett, Josiah, 110
Child, Lydia Maria Francis, 61
Dickens, Charles, 16
Franklin, Benjamin, 87
Garfield, James A., 25
Henry, Patrick, 87
Hopkinson, Francis, 117
Jefferson, Thomas, 140
Lincoln, Abraham, 6
Longstreet, General James, 20
Luther, Martin, 6
Porter, Jane, 15
Rush, Benjamin, 117, 124
Washington, George, 16, 87
Whately, Richard, 10
Wiggin, Kate Douglas, 17
Wilson, James, 117

Recipes (see cooking)

Signers of the Declaration of Independence
Adams, John, 96, 139
Adams, Samuel, 72
Bartlett, Josiah, 110
Braxton, Carter, 90
Carroll, Charles of Carrollton, 102
Chase, Samuel, 113

Index

Clark, Abraham, 105
Clymer, George, 110
Ellery, William, 79
Floyd, William, 66
Franklin, Benjamin, 21
Gerry, Elbridge, 108
Gwinnett, Button, 79
Hall, Lyman, 109
Hancock, John, 104
Harrison, Benjamin, 112
Hart, John, 90
Hewes, Joseph, 83
Heyward Jr., Thomas, 141
Hooper, William, 122
Hopkins, Stephen, 71
Hopkinson, Francis, 113
Huntington, Samuel, 73
Jefferson, Thomas, 140
Lee, Francis Lightfoot, 128
Lee, Richard Henry, 134
Lewis, Francis, 67
Livingston, Philip, 68
Lynch Jr., Thomas, 129
McKean, Thomas, 99
Middleton, Arthur, 128
Morris, Lewis, 78
Morris, Robert, 130
Morton, John, 96
Nelson Jr., Thomas, 116
Paca, William, 92
Paine, Robert Treat, 91
Penn, John, 71
Read, George, 89
Rodney, Caesar, 83
Ross, George, 109
Rush, Benjamin, 123
Rutledge, Edward, 135
Sherman, Roger, 84
Smith, James, 122
Stockton, Richard, 100
Stone, Thomas, 95
Taylor, George, 105
Thornton, Matthew, 114
Walton, George, 96
Whipple, William, 102
Williams, William, 86
Wilson, James, 129
Witherspoon, John, 101
Wolcott, Oliver, 85
Wythe, George, 133

Songs
"America the Beautiful," 118
"My Country 'Tis of Thee," 137
"The Star Spangled Banner," 48
"Yankee Doodle," 75

Stories
"Borrowed Mothers" by Carolyn Sherwin Bailey, 3
"Bravery Honored by a Foe" by Ben La Bree, 20
"Bravery of Richard Kirtland" by Ben La Bree, 21
"Burning Her House" by Celina Eliza Means, 92
"Cornelia's Jewels" by James Baldwin, 15
"Earning the Flag" by Carolyn Sherwin Bailey, 45
"Emily Geiger's Ride" by Benson John Lossing, 98
"An Escape from a Prison Ship" by Everett Titsworth Tomlinson, 126
"A Famous Writing Desk" by Albert Blaisdell, 65
"Flag of Betsy Ross" by Harry Pringle Ford, 43
"The Flag of Their Regiment" by Carolyn Sherwin Bailey, 70
"The General's Daughter" by James Johonnot, 77
"Gold in the Bread" by Albert Blaisdell, 107
"How the Home was Built" by Maud Lindsay, 51
"John Paul Jones" by Albert Blaisdell, 103
"Letter to His Son" by Theodore Roosevelt, 58
"The Little Victory" by Dorothea Lay, 42
"The Midnight Ride of Paul Revere" by Henry Wadsworth Longfellow and Albert Blaisdell 82
"On the Track of a Traitor" by Charles Morris, 111
"The Only Son of His Mother" by Florence Morse Kingsley, 8
"Our Flag's First Engagement" by H. A. Ogden, 37
"The Parshley Celebration" by Sarah Orne Jewett, 29
"The Prodigal Son" retold by Jesse Lyman Hurlbut, 61
"Putnam's Dashing Ride" by James Baldwin, 94
"The Quaker Patriot" by Charles Morris, 89
"The Rescue of a Redcoat" by Grace E. Craig, 119
"The Rescue of Old Glory" by Mrs. J. W. Wheeler, 138
"The Story of William Tell" by James Hiram Fassett, 56
"Tempe Hides Her Horse" by Mr. Blaisdell and Mr. Ball, 78
"Tench Tilghman's Ride" by Jams Baldwin, 132
"Three in a Gully" by Arthur Willis Colton, 22
"Two Heroes of the Civil War" by Ben La Bree, 19
"The Two Windows" by Carolyn Sherwin Bailey, 16
"The Wise Father" by Ernest Clark Hartwell, 62

www.ingramcontent.com/pod-product-compliance
Lightning Source LLC
Chambersburg PA
CBHW051411070526
44584CB00023B/3384